ESSENTIAL BEETON

edited by Alastair Williams

ISABELLA BEETON

summersdale

Essential Beeton
Isabella Beeton
Edited by Alastair Williams

This edition © Summersdale Publishers Ltd 2004

Summersdale Publishers Ltd
46 West Street
Chichester
West Sussex
PO19 1RP
UK

www.summersdale.com

Printed and bound in Great Britain.

ISBN 1 84024 416 X

CONTENTS

PREFACE

I must frankly own, that if I had known, beforehand, that this book would have cost me the labour which it has, I should never have been courageous enough to commence it. What moved me, in the first instance, to attempt a work like this, was the discomfort and suffering which I had seen brought upon men and women by household mismanagement. I have always thought that there is no more fruitful source of family discontent than a housewife's badly-cooked dinners and untidy ways. Men are now so well served out of doors,—at their clubs, well-ordered taverns, and dining-houses, that in order to compete with the attractions of these places, a mistress must be thoroughly acquainted with the theory and practice of cookery, as well as be perfectly conversant with all the other arts of making and keeping a comfortable home.

In this book I have attempted to give, under the chapters devoted to cookery, an intelligible arrangement to every recipe, a list of the *ingredients*, a plain statement of the *mode* of preparing each dish, and a careful estimate of its *cost*, the *number of people* for whom it is *sufficient*, and the time when it is *seasonable*. For the matter of the recipes, I am indebted, in some measure, to many correspondents of the "Englishwoman's Domestic Magazine," who have obligingly placed at my disposal their formulas for many original preparations. A large private circle has also rendered me considerable service. A diligent study of the works of the best modern writers on cookery was also necessary to the faithful fulfilment of my task. Friends in England, Scotland, Ireland, France, and Germany, have also very materially aided me. I have paid great attention to those recipes which come under the head of "COLD MEAT COOKERY." But in the department belonging to the cook I have striven, too, to make my work something more than a Cookery Book, and have, therefore, on the best authority that I could obtain, given an account of the natural history of the animals and vegetables which we use as food. I have followed the animal from his birth to his appearance on the table; have described the manner of feeding him, and of slaying him, the position of his various joints, and, after giving the recipes, have described the modes of carving Meat, Poultry, and Game. Skilful artists have designed the numerous drawings which appear in this work, and which illustrate, better than any description, many important and interesting items.

I wish here to acknowledge the kind letters and congratulations I have received during the progress of this work, and have only further to add, that I trust the result of the four years' incessant labour which I have expended will not be altogether unacceptable to some of my countrymen and countrywomen.

ISABELLA BEETON

INTRODUCTION

The original, and almost certainly unrivalled, domestic goddess Isabella Beeton brought the art of successful home management to the Victorian masses. She worked tirelessly during her short life to provide the nineteenth century middle classes with what were considered to be essential domestic management skills of the day.

The first edition of the mammoth tome *Beeton's Household Management* was published in 1861 by her husband Samuel. This culinary and domestic bible, for which Isabella Beeton is still celebrated today, is the amalgamation of 24 monthly editions of the *English Woman's Domestic Magazine*, produced between 1859 and 1861.

Her mission was to educate people to live, as she put it, 'economically, tastefully and well'. Mrs Beeton's guide is crammed with numerous ideas, from how to employ and treat the servants to knocking together a prawn soup or hashed goose. Taste and etiquette are accounted for in the form of helpful instructions on how to make a pomade for the hair, renew velvet and clean jewellery. The economics of household management are also meticulously detailed; for a nineteenth century readership, the apparently lavish recipe and entertainment suggestions in fact successfully combined good living with economy.

Although twenty-first century society appears to have learnt little from Isabella Beeton's wise words when it comes to manners and etiquette, many of her tried and tested recipes can still be enjoyed today. The advent of the celebrity chef and subsequent cookbooks pay little heed to traditional recipes for practical, everyday foods such as cakes, pies and gravies. In this collection you will find the very best of Isabella Beeton's recipes and tips, offering useful advice, such as how to make the perfect stock, as well as fun and downright absurd suggestions, including how to dress a sheep's head. Britain's archetypal agony aunt even presents some age-old health and beauty hints; for example, the unmissable sections on how to apply leeches and how to promote hair growth.

For a timeless manual on all things domestic, Mrs Beeton's book continues to reign.

ALASTAIR WILLIAMS

GOLDEN RULES FOR THE KITCHEN

Without *cleanliness* and *punctuality* good
Cooking is *impossible*.
Leave nothing *dirty; clean and clear as you go*.
A time for everything, and *everything in time*.
A good Cook *wastes nothing*.
An hour *lost in the morning* has to be run after *all day*.
Haste *without hurry* saves worry, fuss and flurry.
Stew *boiled* is Stew *spoiled*.
Strong fire for *Roasting; clear* fire for *Broiling*.
Wash Vegetables in *three* waters.
Boil fish *quickly*, meat *slowly*.

EXPLANATION OF FRENCH TERMS USED IN MODERN HOUSEHOLD COOKERY

ASPIC.—A savoury jelly, used as an exterior moulding for cold game, poultry, fish, &c. This, being of a transparent nature, allows the bird which it covers to be seen through it. This may also be used for decorating or garnishing.

ASSIETTE (plate).—*Assiettes* are the small *entrées* and *hors-d'oeuvres*, the quantity of which does not exceed what a plate will hold. At dessert, fruits, cheese, chestnuts, biscuits, &c., if served upon a plate, are termed *assiettes*.

ASSIETTE VOLANTE is a dish which a servant hands round to the guests, but is not placed upon the table. Small cheese soufflés and different dishes, which ought to be served very hot, are frequently made *assiettes volantes*.

AU-BLEU.—Fish dressed in such a manner as to have a *bluish* appearance.

BAIN-MARIE.—An open saucepan or kettle of nearly boiling water, in which a smaller vessel can be set for cooking and warming. This is very useful for keeping articles hot, without altering their quantity or quality. If you keep sauce, broth, or soup by the fireside, the soup reduces and becomes too strong, and the sauce thickens as well as reduces; but this is prevented by using the *bain-marie*, in which the water should be very hot, but not boiling.

BÉCHAMEL.—French white sauce, now frequently used in English cookery.

BLANCH.—To whiten poultry, vegetables, fruit, &c., by plunging them into boiling water for a short time, and afterwards plunging them into cold water, there to remain until they are cold.

BLANQUETTE.—A sort of fricassee.

BOUILLI.—Beef or other meat boiled; but, generally speaking, boiled beef is understood by the term.

BOUILLIE.—A French dish resembling hasty-pudding.

BOUILLON.—A thin broth or soup.

BRAISE.—To stew meat with fat bacon until it is tender, it having previously been blanched.

BRAISIÈRE.—A saucepan having a lid with ledges, to put fire on the top.

BRIDER.—To pass a packthread through poultry, game, &c., to keep together their members.

CARAMEL (burnt sugar).—This is made with a piece of sugar, of the size of a nut, browned in the bottom of a saucepan; upon which a cupful of stock is gradually poured, stirring all the time a glass of broth, little by little. It may be used with the feather of a quill, to colour meats, such as the upper part of fricandeaux; and to impart colour to sauces. Caramel made with water instead of stock may be used to colour *compôtes* and other *entremets*.

CASSEROLE.—A crust of rice, which, after having been moulded into the form of a pie, is baked, and then filled with a fricassee of white meat or a purée of game.

COMPÔTE.—A stew, as of fruit or pigeons.

CONSOMMÉ.—Rich stock, or gravy.

CROQUETTE.—Ball of fried rice or potatoes.

CROUTONS.—Sippets of bread.

DAUBIÈRE.—An oval stewpan, in which *daubes* are cooked; *daubes* being meat or fowl stewed in sauce.

DÉSOSSER.—To *bone*, or take out the bones from poultry, game, or fish. This is an operation requiring considerable experience.

ENTRÉES.—Small side or corner dishes, served with the first course.

ENTREMETS.—Small side or corner dishes, served with the second course.

ESCALOPES.—Collops; small, round, thin pieces of tender meat, or of fish, beaten with the handle of a strong knife to make them tender.

FEUILLETAGE.—Puff-paste.

FLAMBER.—To singe fowl or game, after they have been picked.

FONCER.—To put in the bottom of a saucepan slices of ham, veal, or thin broad slices of bacon.

GALETTE.—A broad thin cake.

GÂTEAU.—A cake, correctly speaking; but used sometimes to denote a pudding and a kind of tart.

GLACER.—To glaze, or spread upon hot meats, or larded fowl, a thick and rich sauce or gravy, called *glaze*. This is laid on with a feather or brush, and in confectionery the term means to ice fruits and pastry with sugar, which glistens on hardening.

HORS-D'OEUVRES.—Small dishes, or *assiettes volantes* of sardines, anchovies, and other relishes of this kind, served to the guests during the first course.

LIT.—A bed or layer; articles in thin slices are placed in layers, other articles, or seasoning, being laid between them.

MAIGRE.—Broth, soup, or gravy, made without meat.

MATELOTE.—A rich fish-stew, which is generally composed of carp, eels, trout, or barbel. It is made with wine.

MAYONNAISE.—Cold sauce, or salad dressing.

MENU.—The bill of fare.

MERINGUE.—A kind of icing, made of whites of eggs and sugar, well beaten.

MIROTON.—Larger slices of meat than collops; such as slices of beef for a vinaigrette, or ragout or stew of onions.

MOUILLER.—To add water, broth, or other liquid, during the cooking.

PANER.—To cover over with very fine crumbs of bread, meats, or any other articles to be cooked on the gridiron, in the oven, or frying-pan.

PIQUER.—To lard with strips of fat bacon, poultry, game, meat, &c. This should always be done according to the vein of the meat, so that in carving you slice the bacon across as well as the meat.

POÊLÉE.—Stock used instead of water for boiling turkeys, sweetbreads, fowls, and vegetables, to render them less insipid. This is rather an expensive preparation.

PURÉE.—Vegetables, or meat reduced to a very smooth pulp, which is afterwards mixed with enough liquid to make it of the consistency of very thick soup.

RAGOÛT.—Stew or hash.

REMOULADE.—Salad dressing.

RISSOLES.—Pastry, made of light puff-paste, and cut into various forms, and fried. They may be filled with fish, meat, or sweets.

ROUX.—Brown and white; French thickening.

SALMI.—Ragout of game previously roasted.

SAUCE PIQUANTE.—A sharp sauce, in which somewhat of a vinegar flavour predominates.

SAUTER.—To dress with sauce in a saucepan, repeatedly moving it about.

TAMIS.—Tammy, a sort of open cloth or sieve through which to strain broth and sauces, so as to rid them of small bones, froth, &c.

TOURTE.—Tart. Fruit pie.

TROUSSER.—To truss a bird; to put together the body and tie the wings and thighs, in order to round it for roasting or boiling, each being tied then with packthread, to keep it in the required form.

VOL-AU-VENT.—A rich crust of very fine puff-paste, which may be filled with various delicate ragouts or fricassees, of fish, flesh, or fowl. Fruit may also be inclosed in a *vol-au-vent*.

CHAPTER ONE

RECIPES FOR SOUPS

STOCKS FOR ALL KINDS OF SOUPS

MEDIUM STOCK

Ingredients.—4 lbs. of shin of beef, or 4 lbs. of knuckle of veal, or 2 lbs. of each; any bones, trimmings of poultry, or fresh meat, ½ lb. of lean bacon or ham, 2 oz. of butter, 2 large onions, each stuck with 3 cloves; 1 turnip, 3 carrots, ½ a leek, 1 head of celery, 2 oz. of salt, ½ teaspoonful of whole pepper, 1 large blade of mace, 1 small bunch of savoury herbs, 4 quarts and ½ pint of cold water.

Mode.—Cut up the meat and bacon or ham into pieces about 3 inches square; rub the butter on the bottom of the stewpan; put in ½ pint of water, the meat, and all the other ingredients. Cover the stewpan, and place it on a sharp fire, occasionally stirring its contents. When the bottom of the pan becomes covered with a pale, jelly-like substance, add 4 quarts of cold water, and simmer very gently for 5 hours. As we have said before, do not let it boil quickly. Skim off every particle of grease whilst it is doing, and strain it through a fine hair sieve.

This is the basis of many of the soups afterwards mentioned, and will be found quite strong enough for ordinary purposes.

Time.—5½ hours.

Average cost.—9d. per quart.

RICH STRONG STOCK

Ingredients.—4 lbs. of shin of beef, 4 lbs. of knuckle of veal, ¾ lb. of good lean ham; any poultry trimmings; 3 small onions, 3 small carrots, 3 turnips (the latter should be omitted in summer, lest they ferment), 1 head of celery, a few chopped mushrooms, when obtainable; 1 tomato, a bunch of savoury herbs, not forgetting parsley; 1½ oz. of salt, 12 white peppercorns, 6 cloves, 3 small blades of mace, 4 quarts of water.

Mode.—Line a delicately clean stewpan with the ham cut in thin broad slices, carefully trimming off all its rusty fat; cut up the beef and veal in pieces about 3 inches square, and lay them on the ham; set it on the stove, and draw it down, and stir frequently. When the meat is equally browned, put in the beef and veal bones, the poultry trimmings, and pour in the cold water. Skim well, and occasionally add a little cold water, to stop its boiling, until it becomes quite clear; then put in all the other ingredients, and simmer very slowly for 5 hours. Do not let it come to a brisk boil, that the stock be not wasted, and that its colour may be preserved. Strain through a very fine hair sieve, or tammy, and it will be fit for use.

Time.—5 hours.

Average cost.—1s. 3d. per quart.

WHITE STOCK
(To be Used in the Preparation of White Soups)

Ingredients.—4 lbs. of knuckle of veal, any poultry trimmings, 4 slices of lean ham, 1 carrot, 2 onions, 1 head of celery, 12 white peppercorns, 1 oz. of salt, 1 blade of mace, 1 oz. of butter, 4 quarts of water.

Mode.—Cut up the veal, and put it with the bones and trimmings of poultry, and the ham, into the stewpan, which has been rubbed with the butter. Moisten with ½ pint of water, and simmer till the gravy begins to flow. Then add the 4 quarts of water and the remainder of the ingredients; simmer for 5 hours. After skimming and straining it carefully through a very fine hair sieve, it will be ready for use.

Time.—5½ hours.

Average cost.—9d. per quart.

Note.—When stronger stock is desired, double the quantity of veal, or put in an old fowl. The liquor in which a young turkey has been boiled is an excellent addition to all white stock or soups.

ALMOND SOUP

Ingredients.—4 lbs. of lean beef or veal, ½ a scrag of mutton, 1 oz. of vermicelli, 4 blades of mace, 6 cloves, ½ lb. of sweet almonds, the yolks of 6 eggs, 1 gill of thick cream, rather more than 2 quarts of water.

Mode.—Boil the beef, or veal, and the mutton, gently in water that will cover them, till the gravy is very strong, and the meat very tender; then strain off the gravy, and set it on the fire with the specified quantities of vermicelli, mace, and cloves, to 2 quarts. Let it boil till it has the flavour of the spices. Have ready the almonds, blanched and pounded very fine; the yolks of the eggs boiled hard; mixing the almonds, whilst pounding, with a little of the soup, lest the latter should grow oily. Pound them till they are a mere pulp, and keep adding to them, by degrees, a little soup until they are thoroughly mixed together. Let the soup be cool when mixing, and do it perfectly smooth. Strain it through a sieve, set it on the fire, stir frequently, and serve hot. Just before taking it up, add the cream.

Time.—3 hours.
Average cost per quart.—2s. 3d.
Seasonable all the year.
Sufficient for 8 persons.

The Almond Tree.—This tree is indigenous to the northern parts of Asia and Africa, but it is now cultivated in Europe, especially in the south of France, Italy, and Spain. It flowers in spring, and produces its fruit in August. Although there are two kinds of almonds, the *sweet* and the *bitter,* they are considered as only varieties of the same species. The best sweet almonds brought to England, are called the Syrian or Jordan, and come from Malaga; the inferior qualities are brought from Valentia and Italy. *Bitter* almonds come principally from Magadore. Anciently, the almond was much esteemed by the nations of the East. Jacob included it among the presents which he designed for Joseph. The Greeks called it the Greek or Thasian nut, and the Romans believed that by eating half a dozen of them, they were secured against drunkenness, however deeply they might imbibe. Almonds, however, are considered as very indigestible. The *bitter* contain, too, principles which produce two violent poisons,—prussic acid and a kind of volatile oil. It is consequently dangerous to eat them in large quantities. Almonds pounded together with a little sugar and water, however, produce a milk similar to that which is yielded by animals. Their oil is used for making fine soap, and their cake as a cosmetic.

ALMOND AND
BLOSSOM.

BARLEY SOUP

Ingredients.—2 lbs. of shin of beef, ¼ lb. of pearl barley, a large bunch of parsley, 4 onions, 6 potatoes, salt and pepper, 4 quarts of water.

Mode.—Put in all the ingredients, and simmer gently for 3 hours.

Time.—3 hours.

Average cost.—2½d. per quart.

Seasonable all the year, but more suitable for winter.

BARLEY.

Barley.—This, in the order of cereal grasses, is, in Britain, the next plant to wheat in point of value, and exhibits several species and varieties. From what country it comes originally, is not known, but it was cultivated in the earliest ages of antiquity, as the Egyptians were afflicted with the loss of it in the ear, in the time of Moses. It was a favourite grain with the Athenians, but it was esteemed as an ignominious food by the Romans. Notwithstanding this, however, it was much used by them, as it was in former times by the English, and still is, in the Border counties, in Cornwall, and also in Wales. In other parts of England, it is used mostly for malting purposes. It is less nutritive than wheat; and in 100 parts, has of starch 79, gluten 6, saccharine matter 7, husk 8. It is, however, a lighter and less stimulating food than wheat, which renders a decoction of it well adapted for invalids whose digestion is weak.

26

PEA SOUP (GREEN)

Ingredients.—3 pints of green peas, ¼ lb. of butter, 2 or 3 thin slices of ham, 6 onions sliced, 4 shredded lettuces, the crumb of 2 French rolls, 2 handfuls of spinach, 1 lump of sugar, 2 quarts of common stock.

Mode.—Put the butter, ham, 1 quart of the peas, onions, and lettuces, to a pint of stock, and simmer for an hour; then add the remainder of the stock, with the crumb of the French rolls, and boil for another hour. Now boil the spinach, and squeeze it very dry. Rub the soup through a sieve, and the spinach with it, to colour it. Have ready a pint of *young* peas boiled; add them to the soup, put in the sugar, give one boil, and serve. If necessary, add salt.

Time.—2½ hours.

Average cost.—1s. 9d. per quart.

Seasonable from June to the end of August.

Sufficient for 10 persons.

Note.—It will be well to add, if the peas are not quite young, a little sugar. Where economy is essential, water may be used instead of stock for this soup, boiling in it likewise the pea-shells; but use a double quantity of vegetables.

SPINACH SOUP

(French Recipe)

Ingredients.—As much spinach as, when boiled, will half fill a vegetable-dish, 2 quarts of very clear medium stock.

Mode.—Make the cooked spinach into balls the size of an egg, and slip them into the soup-tureen. This is a very elegant soup, the green of the spinach forming a pretty contrast to the brown gravy.

Time.—1 hour.

Average cost.—1s. per quart.

Seasonable from October to June.

SPINACH.

Spinach.—This plant was unknown by the ancients, although it was cultivated in the monastic gardens of the continent in the middle of the 14th century. Some say, that it was originally brought from Spain; but there is a wild species growing in England, and cultivated in Lincolnshire, in preference to the other. There are three varieties in use; the round-leaved, the triangular-leaved, and Flanders spinach, known by its large leaves. They all form a useful ingredient in soup; but the leaves are sometimes boiled alone, mashed, and eaten as greens.

VEGETABLE MARROW SOUP

Ingredients.—4 young vegetable marrows, or more, if very small, ½ pint of cream, salt and white pepper to taste, 2 quarts of white stock.

Mode.—Pare and slice the marrows, and put them in the stock boiling. When done almost to a mash, press them through a sieve, and at the moment of serving, add the boiling cream and seasoning.

Time.—1 hour.

Average cost.—1s. 2d. per quart.

Seasonable in summer.

Sufficient for 8 persons.

VEGETABLE-MARROW.

The Vegetable Marrow.—This is a variety of the gourd family, brought from Persia by an East-India ship, and only recently introduced to Britain. It is already cultivated to a considerable extent, and, by many, is highly esteemed when fried with butter. It is, however, dressed in different ways, either by stewing or boiling, and, besides, made into pies.

HESSIAN SOUP

Ingredients.—½ an ox's head, 1 pint of split peas, 3 carrots, 6 turnips, 6 potatoes, 6 onions, 1 head of celery, 1 bunch of savoury herbs, pepper and salt to taste, 2 blades of mace, a little allspice, 4 cloves, the crumb of a French roll, 6 quarts of water.

Mode.—Clean the head, rub it with salt and water, and soak it for 5 hours in warm water. Simmer it in the water till tender, put it into a pan and let it cool; skim off all the fat; take out the head, and add the vegetables cut up small, and the peas which have been previously soaked; simmer them without the meat, till they are done enough to pulp through a sieve. Add the seasoning, with pieces of the meat cut up; give one boil, and serve.

Time.—4 hours.

Average cost.—6d. per quart.

Seasonable in winter.

Sufficient for 16 persons.

Note.—An excellent hash or *ragoût* can be made by cutting up the nicest parts of the head, thickening and seasoning more highly a little of the soup, and adding a glass of port wine and 2 tablespoonfuls of ketchup.

MOCK TURTLE

Ingredients.—A knuckle of veal weighing 5 or 6 lbs., 2 cow-heels, 2 large onions stuck with cloves, 1 bunch of sweet herbs, 3 blades of mace, salt to taste, 12 peppercorns, 1 glass of sherry, 24 forcemeat balls, a little lemon-juice, 4 quarts of water.

Mode.—Put all the ingredients, except the forcemeat balls and lemon-juice, in an earthen jar, and stew for 6 hours. Do not open it till cold. When wanted for use, skim off all the fat, and strain carefully; place it on the fire, cut up the meat into inch-and-a-half squares, put it, with the forcemeat balls and lemon-juice, into the soup, and serve. It can be flavoured with a tablespoonful of anchovy, or Harvey's sauce.

Time.—6 hours.

Average cost.—1s. 4d. per quart.

Seasonable in winter.

Sufficient for 10 persons.

The Calf.—The flesh of this animal is called veal, and when young, that is, under two months old, yields a large quantity of soluble extract, and is, therefore, much employed for soups and broths. The Essex farmers have obtained a celebrity for fattening calves better than any others in England, where they are plentifully supplied with milk, a thing impossible to be done in the immediate neighbourhood of London.

A GOOD FAMILY SOUP

Ingredients.—Remains of a cold tongue, 2 lbs. of shin of beef, any cold pieces of meat or beef-bones, 2 turnips, 2 carrots, 2 onions, 1 parsnip, 1 head of celery, 4 quarts of water, ½ teacupful of rice, salt and pepper to taste.

Mode.—Put all the ingredients in a stewpan, and simmer gently for 4 hours, or until all the goodness is drawn from the meat. Strain off the soup, and let it stand to get cold. The kernels and soft parts of the tongue must be saved. When the soup is wanted for use, skim off all the fat, put in the kernels and soft parts of the tongue, slice in a small quantity of fresh carrot, turnip, and onion; stew till the vegetables are tender, and serve with toasted bread.

Time.—5 hours.

Average cost.—3d. per quart.

Seasonable at any time.

Sufficient for 12 persons.

FISH SOUPS

EEL SOUP

Ingredients.—3 lbs. of eels, 1 onion, 2 oz. of butter, 3 blades of mace, 1 bunch of sweet herbs, ¼ oz. of peppercorns, salt to taste, 2 tablespoonfuls of flour, ¼ pint of cream, 2 quarts of water.

Mode.—Wash the eels, cut them into thin slices, and put them in the stewpan with the butter; let them simmer for a few minutes, then pour the water to them, and add the onion, cut in thin slices, the herbs, mace, and seasoning. Simmer till the eels are tender, but do not break the fish. Take them out carefully, mix the flour smoothly to a batter with the cream, bring it to a boil, pour over the eels, and serve.

Time.—1 hour, or rather more.

Average cost.—10d. per quart.

Seasonable from June to March.

Sufficient for 8 persons.

Note.—This soup may be flavoured differently by omitting the cream, and adding a little ketchup cr Harvey's sauce.

PRAWN SOUP

Ingredients.—2 quarts of fish stock or water, 2 pints of prawns, the crumb of a French roll, anchovy sauce or mushroom ketchup to taste, 1 blade of mace, 1 pint of vinegar, a little lemon-juice.

Mode.—Pick out the tails of the prawns, put the bodies in a stewpan with 1 blade of mace, ½ pint of vinegar, and the same quantity of water; stew them for ¼ hour, and strain off the liquor. Put the fish stock or water into a stewpan; add the strained liquor, pound the prawns with the crumb of a roll moistened with a little of the soup, rub them through a tammy, and mix them by degrees with the soup; add ketchup or anchovy sauce to taste, with a little lemon-juice. When it is well cooked, put in a few picked prawns; let them get thoroughly hot, and serve. If not thick enough, put in a little butter and flour.

Time.—hour.

Average cost.—1s. 1d. per quart, if made with water.

Seasonable at any time.

Sufficient for 8 persons.

Note.—This can be thickened with tomatoes, and vermicelli served in it, which makes it a very tasteful soup.

CHAPTER TWO

RECIPES FOR COOKING FISH

BOILED EELS

Ingredients.—4 small eels, sufficient water to cover them; a large bunch of parsley.

Mode.—Choose small eels for boiling; put them in a stewpan with the parsley, and just sufficient water to cover them; simmer till tender. Take them out, pour a little parsley and butter over them, and serve some in a tureen.

Time.—½ hour.

Average cost.—6d. per lb.

Seasonable from June to March.

Sufficient for 4 persons.

THE EEL.

The Eel Tribe.—The Apodal, or bony-gilled and ventral-finned fish, of which the eel forms the first Linnaean tribe, in their general aspect and manners, approach, in some instances, very nearly to serpents. They have a smooth head and slippery skin, are in general naked, or covered with such small, soft, and distant scales, as are scarcely visible. Their bodies are long and slender, and they are supposed to subsist entirely on animal substances. There are about nine species of them, mostly found in the seas. One of them frequents our fresh waters, and three of the others occasionally pay a visit to our shores.

FISH AND OYSTER PIE

Ingredients.—Any remains of cold fish, such as cod or haddock; 2 dozen oysters, pepper and salt to taste, bread crumbs sufficient for the quantity of fish; ½ teaspoonful of grated nutmeg, 1 teaspoonful of finely-chopped parsley.

Mode.—Clear the fish from the bones, and put a layer of it in a pie-dish, which sprinkle with pepper and salt; then a layer of bread crumbs, oysters, nutmeg, and chopped parsley. Repeat this till the dish is quite full. You may form a covering either of bread crumbs, which should be browned, or puff-paste, which should be cut into long strips, and laid in cross-bars over the fish, with a line of the paste first laid round the edge. Before putting on the top, pour in some made melted butter, or a little thin white sauce, and the oyster-liquor, and bake.

Time.—If made of cooked fish, ¼ hour; if made of fresh fish and puff-paste, ¾ hour.

Average cost.—1s. 6d.

Seasonable from September to April.

Note.—A nice little dish may be made by flaking any cold fish, adding a few oysters, seasoning with pepper and salt, and covering with mashed potatoes; ¼ hour will bake it.

TENCH STEWED WITH WINE

Ingredients.—½ pint of medium stock, ½ pint of Madeira or sherry, salt and pepper to taste, 1 bay-leaf, thickening of butter and flour.

Mode.—Clean and crimp the tench; carefully lay it in a stewpan with the stock, wine, salt and pepper, and bay-leaf; let it stew gently for ½ hour; then take it out, put it on a dish, and keep hot. Strain the liquor, and thicken it with butter and flour kneaded together, and stew for 5 minutes. If not perfectly smooth, squeeze it through a tammy, add a very little cayenne, and pour over the fish. Garnish with balls of veal forcemeat.

Time.—Rather more than ½ hour.

Seasonable from October to June.

TENCH.

STEWED TROUT

Ingredients.—2 middling-sized trout, ½ onion cut in thin slices, a little parsley, 2 cloves, 1 blade of mace, 2 bay-leaves, a little thyme, salt and pepper to taste, 1 pint of medium stock, 1 glass of port wine, thickening of butter and flour.

Mode.—Wash the fish very clean, and wipe it quite dry. Lay it in a stewpan, with all the ingredients but the butter and flour, and simmer gently for ½ hour, or rather more, should not the fish be quite done. Take it out, strain the gravy, add the thickening, and stir it over a sharp fire for 5 minutes; pour it over the trout, and serve.

Time.—According to size, ½ hour or more.

Average cost.—Seldom bought.

Seasonable from May to September, and fatter from the middle to the end of August than at any other time.

Sufficient for 4 persons.

Trout may be served with anchovy or caper sauce, baked in buttered paper, or fried whole like smelts.

THE TROUT.

CARVING SALMON

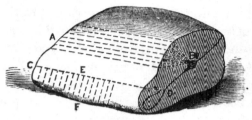

SALMON.

First run the knife quite down to the bone, along the side of the fish, from *A* to *B*, and also from *C* to *D*. Then help the thick part lengthwise, that is, in the direction of the lines from *A* to *B*; and the thin part breadthwise, that is, in the direction of the lines from *E* to *F*, as shown in the engraving. A slice of the thick part should always be accompanied by a smaller piece of the thin from the belly, where lies the fat of the fish.

Note.—Many persons, in carving salmon, make the mistake of slicing the thick part of this fish in the opposite direction to that we have stated; and thus, by the breaking of the flakes, the beauty of its appearance is destroyed.

CARVING TURBOT

First run the fish-slice down the thickest part of the fish, quite through to the bone, from *A* to *B*, and then cut handsome and regular slices in the direction of the lines downwards, from *D* to *E*, and upwards from *C* to *D*, as shown in the engraving. When the carver has removed all the meat from the upper side of the fish, the backbone should be raised, put on one side of the dish, and the under side helped as the upper.

A BRILL and JOHN DORY are carved in the same manner as a Turbot.

Note.—The thick parts of the middle of the back are the best slices in a turbot; and the rich gelatinous skin covering the fish, as well as a little of the thick part of the fins, are dainty morsels, and should be placed on each plate.

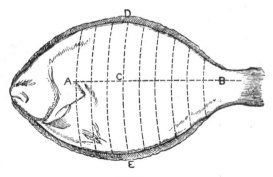

TURBOT.

42

CHAPTER THREE

RECIPES FOR GRAVIES, FORCEMEATS, AND SAUCES

BROWN GRAVY

Ingredients.—2 oz of butter, 2 large onions, 2 lbs. of shin of beef, 2 small slices of lean bacon (if at hand), salt and whole pepper to taste, 3 cloves, 2 quarts of water. For thickening, 2 oz. of butter, 3 oz. of flour.

Mode.—Put the butter into a stewpan; set this on the fire, throw in the onions cut in rings, and fry them a light brown; then add the beef and bacon, which should be cut into small square pieces; season, and pour in a teacupful of water; let it boil for about 10 minutes, or until it is of a nice brown colour, occasionally stirring the contents. Now fill up with water in the above proportion; let it boil up, when draw it to the side of the fire to simmer very gently for 1½ hour; strain, and when cold, take off all the fat. In thickening this gravy, melt 3 oz. of butter in a stewpan, add 2 oz. of flour, and stir till of a light-brown colour; when cold, add it to the strained gravy, and boil it up quickly. This thickening may be made in larger quantities, and kept in a stone jar for use when wanted.

Time.—Altogether, 2 hours.

Average cost.—4d. per pint.

GRAVY FOR VENISON

Ingredients.—Trimmings of venison, 3 or 4 mutton shank-bones, salt to taste, 1 pint of water, 2 teaspoonfuls of walnut ketchup.

Mode.—Brown the trimmings over a nice clear fire, and put them in a stewpan with the shank-bones and water; simmer gently for 2 hours, strain and skim, and add the walnut ketchup and a seasoning of salt. Let it just boil, when it is ready to serve.

Time.—2 hours.

FORCEMEAT FOR COLD SAVOURY PIES

Ingredients.—1 lb. of veal, 1 lb. of fat bacon; salt, cayenne, pepper, and pounded mace to taste; a very little nutmeg, the same of chopped lemon-peel, ½ teaspoonful of chopped parsley, ½ teaspoonful of minced savoury herbs, 1 or 2 eggs.

Mode.—Chop the veal and bacon together, and put them in a mortar with the other ingredients mentioned above. Pound well, and bind with 1 or 2 eggs which have been previously beaten and strained. Work the whole well together, and the forcemeat will be ready for use. If the pie is not to be eaten immediately, omit the herbs and parsley, as these would prevent it from keeping. Mushrooms or truffles may be added.

Sufficient for 2 small pies.

MARJORAM.

Marjoram.—Although there are several species of marjoram, that which is known as the sweet or knotted marjoram, is the one usually preferred in cookery. It is a native of Portugal, and when its leaves are used as a seasoning herb, they have an agreeable aromatic flavour. The winter sweet marjoram used for the same purposes, is a native of Greece, and the pot-marjoram is another variety brought from Sicily. All of them are favourite ingredients in soups, stuffings, &c.

BOILED CALF'S UDDER FOR FRENCH FORCEMEATS

Put the udder into a stewpan with sufficient water to cover it; let it stew gently till quite done, when take it out to cool. Trim all the upper parts, cut it into small pieces, and pound well in a mortar, till it can be rubbed through a sieve. That portion which passes through the strainer is one of the three ingredients of which French forcemeats are generally composed; but many cooks substitute butter for this, being a less troublesome and more expeditious mode of preparation.

PESTLE AND MORTAR.

Pestle and Mortar.—No cookery can be perfectly performed without the aid of the useful instruments shown in the engraving. For pounding things sufficiently fine, they are invaluable, and the use of them will save a good deal of time, besides increasing the excellence of the preparations. They are made of iron, and, in that material, can be bought cheap; but as these are not available, for all purposes, we should recommend, as more economical in the end, those made of Wedgwood, although these are considerably more expensive than the former.

SAUSAGE-MEAT STUFFING, for Turkey

Ingredients.—6 oz. of lean pork, 6 oz. of fat pork, both weighed after being chopped (beef suet may be substituted for the latter), 2 oz. of bread crumbs, 1 small tablespoonful of minced sage, 1 blade of pounded mace, salt and pepper to taste, 1 egg.

Mode.—Chop the meat and fat very finely, mix with them the other ingredients, taking care that the whole is thoroughly incorporated. Moisten with the egg, and the stuffing will be ready for use. Equal quantities of this stuffing and forcemeat will be found to answer very well, as the herbs, lemon-peel, &c. in the latter, impart a very delicious flavour to the sausage-meat. As preparations, however, like stuffings and forcemeats, are matters to be decided by individual tastes, they must be left, to a great extent, to the discrimination of the cook, who should study her employer's taste in this, as in every other respect.

Average cost.—9d.

Sufficient for a small turkey.

GENERAL REMARKS ON SAUCES

AN ANECDOTE IS TOLD of the prince de Soubise, who, intending to give an entertainment, asked for the bill of fare. His *chef* came, presenting a list adorned with vignettes, and the first article of which, that met the prince's eye, was "fifty hams." "Bertrand," said the prince, "I think you must be extravagant; Fifty hams! do you intend to feast my whole regiment?" "No, Prince, there will be but one on the table, and the surplus I need for my Espagnole, blondes, garnitures, &c." "Bertrand, you are robbing me: this item will not do." "Monseigneur," said the *artiste*, "you do not appreciate me. Give me the order, and I will put those fifty hams in a crystal flask no longer than my thumb." The prince smiled, and the hams were passed. This was all very well for the prince de Soubise; but as we do not write for princes and nobles alone, but that our British sisters may make the best dishes out of the least expensive ingredients, we will also pass the hams, and give a few general directions concerning Sauces, &c.

ANCHOVY SAUCE

Ingredients.—4 anchovies, 1 oz. of butter, ½ pint of melted butter, cayenne to taste.

Mode.—Bone the anchovies, and pound them in a mortar to a paste, with 1 oz. of butter. Make the melted butter hot, stir in the pounded anchovies and cayenne; simmer for 3 or 4 minutes; and if liked, add a squeeze of lemon-juice. A more general and expeditious way of making this sauce is to stir in 1½ tablespoonfuls of anchovy essence to ½ pint of melted butter, and to add seasoning to taste. Boil the whole up for 1 minute, and serve hot.

Time.—5 minutes.

Average cost.—5d. for ½ pint.

Sufficient, this quantity, for a brill, small turbot, 3 or 4 soles, &c.

THE CAPSICUM.

Cayenne.—This is the most acrid and stimulating spice with which we are acquainted. It is a powder prepared from several varieties of the capsicum annual East-India plants, of which there are three so far naturalised in this country as to be able to grow in the open air: these are the Guinea, the Cherry, and the Bell pepper. All the pods of these are extremely pungent to the taste, and in the green state are used by us as a pickle. When ripe, they are ground into cayenne pepper, and sold as a condiment. The best of this, however, is made in the West Indies, from what is called the *Bird* pepper, on account of hens and turkeys being extremely partial to it. It is imported ready for use. Of the capiscum species of plants there are five; but the principal are,—1. *Capsicum annuum*, the common long-podded capsicum, which is cultivated in our gardens, and of which there are two varieties, one with red, and another with yellow fruit. 2. *Capsicum baccatum*, or bird pepper, which rises with a shrubby stalk four or five feet high, with its berries growing at the division of the branches: this is small, oval-shaped, and of a bright-red colour, from which, as we have said, the best cayenne is made. 3. *Capsicum grossum*, the bell-pepper: the fruit of this is red, and is the only kind fit for pickling.

APPLE SAUCE

Ingredients.—6 good-sized apples, sifted sugar to taste, a piece of butter the size of a walnut, water.

Mode.—Pare, core, and quarter the apples, and throw them into cold water to preserve their whiteness. Put them in a saucepan, with sufficient water to moisten them, and boil till soft enough to pulp. Beat them up, adding sugar to taste, and a small piece of butter. This quantity is sufficient for a good-sized tureen.

Time.—According to the apples, about ¾ hour.

Average cost.—4d.

Sufficient, this quantity, for a goose or couple of ducks.

ASPARAGUS SAUCE

Ingredients.—1 bunch of green asparagus, salt, 1 oz. of fresh butter, 1 small bunch of parsley, 3 or 4 green onions, 1 large lump of sugar, 4 tablespoonfuls of sauce tournée.

Mode.—Break the asparagus in the tender part, wash well, and put them into boiling salt and water to render them green. When they are tender, take them out, and put them into cold water; drain them on a cloth till all moisture is absorbed from them. Put the butter in a stewpan, with the parsley and onions; lay in the asparagus, and fry the whole over a sharp fire for 5 minutes. Add salt, the sugar and sauce tournée, and simmer for another 5 minutes. Rub all through a tammy, and if not a very good colour, use a little spinach green. This sauce should be rather sweet.

Time.—Altogether 40 minutes.

Average cost for this quantity, 1s. 4d.

FRENCH WHITE SAUCE

Ingredients.—1 small bunch of parsley, 2 cloves, ½ bay-leaf, 1 small faggot of savoury herbs, salt to taste; 3 or 4 mushrooms, when obtainable; 2 pints of white stock, 1 pint of cream, 1 tablespoonful of arrowroot.

Mode.—Put the stock into a stewpan, with the parsley, cloves, bay-leaf, herbs, and mushrooms; add a seasoning of salt, but no pepper, as that would give the sauce a dusty appearance, and should be avoided. When it has boiled long enough to extract the flavour of the herbs, &c., strain it, and boil it up quickly again, until it is nearly half-reduced. Now mix the arrowroot smoothly with the cream, and let it simmer very gently for 5 minutes over a slow fire; pour to it the reduced stock, and continue to simmer slowly for 10 minutes, if the sauce be thick. If, on the contrary, it be too thin, it must be stirred over a sharp fire till it thickens. This is the foundation of many kinds of sauces, especially white sauces. Always make it thick, as you can easily thin it with cream, milk, or white stock.

Time.—Altogether, 2 hours.

Average cost, 1s. per pint.

The Clove.—The clove-tree is a native of the Molucca Islands, particularly Amboyna, and attains the height of a laurel-tree, and no verdure is ever seen under it. From the extremities of the branches quantities of flowers grow, first white; then they become green, and next red and hard, when they have arrived at their clove state. When they become dry, they assume a yellowish hue, which subsequently changes into a dark brown. As an aromatic, the clove is highly stimulating, and yields an abundance of oil. There are several varieties of the clove; the best is called the *royal clove*, which is scarce, and which is blacker and smaller than the other kinds. It is a curious fact, that the flowers, when fully developed, are quite inodorous, and that the real fruit is not in the least aromatic. The form is that of a nail, having a globular head, formed of the four petals of the corolla, and four leaves of the calyx not expanded, with a nearly cylindrical germen, scarcely an inch in length, situated below.

THE CLOVE.

BREAD SAUCE, *to serve with Roast Turkey, Fowl, Game, &c.*

Ingredients.—1 pint of milk, ¾ of the crumb of a stale loaf, 1 onion; pounded mace, cayenne, and salt to taste; 1 oz. of butter.

Mode.—Peel and quarter the onion, and simmer it in the milk till perfectly tender. Break the bread, which should be stale, into small pieces, carefully picking out any hard outside pieces; put it in a very clean saucepan, strain the milk over it, cover it up, and let it remain for an hour to soak. Now beat it up with a fork very smoothly, add a seasoning of pounded mace, cayenne, and salt, with 1 oz. of butter; give the whole one boil, and serve. To enrich this sauce, a small quantity of cream may be added just before sending it to table.

Time.—Altogether, 1¾ hour.

Average cost for this quantity, 4d.

Sufficient to serve with a turkey, pair of fowls, or brace of partridges.

Mace.—This is the membrane which surrounds the shell of the nutmeg. Its general qualities are the same as those of the nutmeg, producing an agreeable aromatic odour, with a hot and acrid taste. It is of an oleaginous nature, is yellowish in its hue, and is used largely as a condiment.

MACE.

HORSERADISH SAUCE, to serve with Roast Beef

Ingredients.—4 tablespoonfuls of grated horseradish, 1 teaspoonful of pounded sugar, 1 teaspoonful of salt, ½ teaspoonful of pepper, 2 teaspoonfuls of made mustard; vinegar.

Mode.—Grate the horseradish, and mix it well with the sugar, salt, pepper, and mustard; moisten it with sufficient vinegar to give it the consistency of cream, and serve in a tureen: 3 or 4 tablespoonfuls of cream added to the above, very much improve the appearance and flavour of this sauce. To heat it to serve with hot roast beef, put it in a bain-marie or a jar, which place in a saucepan of boiling water; make it hot, but do not allow it to boil, or it will curdle.

Note.—This sauce is a great improvement on the old-fashioned way of serving cold-scraped horseradish with hot roast beef. The mixing of the cold vinegar with the warm gravy cools and spoils everything on the plate. Of course, with cold meat, the sauce should be served cold.

FRENCH SALAD DRESSING

Ingredients.—4 eggs, ½ tablespoonful of made mustard, salt and cayenne to taste, 3 tablespoonfuls of olive-oil, 1 tablespoonful of tarragon or plain vinegar.

Mode.—Boil 3 eggs quite hard for about ¼ hour, put them into cold water, and let them remain in it for a few minutes; strip off the shells, put the yolks in a mortar, and pound them very smoothly; add to them, very gradually, the mustard, seasoning, and vinegar, keeping all well stirred and rubbed down with the back of a wooden spoon. Put in the oil drop by drop, and when this is thoroughly mixed with the other ingredients, add the yolk of a raw egg, and stir well, when it will be ready for use. This sauce should not be curdled; and to prevent this, the only way is to mix a little of everything at a time, and not to cease stirring. The quantities of oil and vinegar may be increased or diminished according to taste, as many persons would prefer a smaller proportion of the former ingredient.

Time.—¼ hour to boil the eggs.

Average cost, for this quantity, 7d.

Sufficient for a salad made for 4 or 6 persons.

VANILLA CUSTARD SAUCE, to serve with Puddings

Ingredients.—½ pint of milk, 2 eggs, 2 oz. of sugar, 10 drops of essence of vanilla.

Mode.—Beat the eggs, sweeten the milk; stir these ingredients well together, and flavour them with essence of vanilla, regulating the proportion of this latter ingredient by the strength of the essence, the size of the eggs, &c. Put the mixture into a small jug, place this jug in a saucepan of boiling water, and stir the sauce *one way* until it thickens; but do not allow it to boil, or it will instantly curdle. Serve in a boat or tureen separately, with plum, bread, or any kind of dry pudding. Essence of bitter almonds or lemon-rind may be substituted for the vanilla, when they are more in accordance with the flavouring of the pudding with which the sauce is intended to be served.

Time.—To be stirred in the jug from 8 to 10 minutes.

Average cost.—4d.

Sufficient for 4 or 5 persons.

WINE OR BRANDY SAUCE FOR PUDDINGS

Ingredients.—½ pint of melted butter, 3 heaped teaspoonfuls of pounded sugar; 1 *large* wineglassful of port or sherry, or ¾ of a *small* glassful of brandy.

Mode.—Make ½ pint of melted butter; then stir in the sugar and wine or spirit in the above proportion, and bring the sauce to the point of boiling. Serve in a boat or tureen separately, and, if liked, pour a little of it over the pudding. To convert this into punch sauce, add to the sherry and brandy a small wineglassful of rum and the juice and grated rind of ½ lemon. Liqueurs, such as Maraschino or Curaçoa substituted for the brandy, make excellent sauces.

Time.—Altogether, 15 minutes.

Average cost.—8d.

Sufficient for 6 or 7 persons.

WHITE SAUCE

(Good)

Ingredients.—½ pint of white stock, ½ pint of cream, 1 dessertspoonful of flour, salt to taste.

Mode.—Have ready a delicately-clean saucepan, into which put the stock, which should be well flavoured with vegetables, and rather savoury; mix the flour smoothly with the cream, add it to the stock, season with a little salt, and boil all these ingredients very gently for about 10 minutes, keeping them well stirred the whole time, as this sauce is very liable to burn.

Time.—10 minutes.

Average cost.—1s.

Sufficient for a pair of fowls.

Seasonable at any time.

BROWN ROUX, a French Thickening for Gravies and Sauces.

Ingredients.—6 oz. of butter, 9 oz. of flour.

Mode.—Melt the butter in a stewpan over a slow fire, and dredge in, very gradually, the flour; stir it till of a light-brown colour—to obtain this do it very slowly, otherwise the flour will burn and impart a bitter taste to the sauce it is mixed with. Pour it in a jar, and keep it for use: it will remain good some time.

Time.—About ½ hour.

Average cost.—7d.

CHAPTER FOUR

RECIPES FOR COOKING BEEF

BAKED BEEF

(Cold Meat Cookery)

Ingredients.—About 2 lbs. of cold roast beef, 2 small onions, 1 large carrot or 2 small ones, 1 turnip, a small bunch of savoury herbs, salt and pepper to taste, 4 tablespoonfuls of gravy, 3 tablespoonfuls of ale, crust or mashed potatoes.

Mode.—Cut the beef in slices, allowing a small amount of fat to each slice; place a layer of this in the bottom of a pie-dish, with a portion of the onions, carrots, and turnips, which must be sliced; mince the herbs, strew them over the meat, and season with pepper and salt. Then put another layer of meat, vegetables, and seasoning; and proceed in this manner until all the ingredients are used. Pour in the gravy and ale (water may be substituted for the former, but it is not so nice), cover with a crust or mashed potatoes, and bake for ½ hour, or rather longer.

Time.—Rather more than ½ hour.

Average cost, exclusive of the meat, 6d.

Sufficient for 5 or 6 persons.

Seasonable at any time.

Note.—It is as well to parboil the carrots and turnips before adding them to the meat, and to use some of the liquor in which they were boiled as a substitute for gravy; that is to say, when there is no gravy at hand. Be particular to cut the onions in very *thin* slices.

BEEF-STEAK PIE

Ingredients.—3 lbs. of rump-steak, seasoning to taste of salt, cayenne, and black pepper; crust, water, the yolk of an egg.

Mode.—Have the steaks cut from a rump that has hung a few days, that they may be tender, and be particular that every portion is perfectly sweet. Cut the steaks into pieces about 3 inches long and 2 wide, allowing a *small* piece of fat to each piece of lean, and arrange the meat in layers in a pie-dish. Between each layer sprinkle a seasoning of salt, pepper, and, when liked, a few grains of cayenne. Fill the dish sufficiently with meat to support the crust, and to give it a nice raised appearance when baked, and not to look flat and hollow. Pour in sufficient water to half fill the dish, and border it with paste; brush it over with a little water, and put on the cover; slightly press down the edges with the thumb, and trim off close to the dish. Ornament the pie with leaves, or pieces of paste cut in any shape that fancy may direct, brush it over with the beaten yolk of an egg; make a hole in the top of the crust, and bake in a hot oven for about 1½ hour.

Time.—In a hot oven, 1½ hour.
Average cost, for this size, 3s 6d.
Sufficient for 6 or 8 persons.
Seasonable at any time.

Note.—Beef-steak pies may be flavoured in various ways, with oysters and their liquor, mushrooms, minced onions, &c. For family pies, suet may be used instead of butter or lard for the crust, and clarified beef-dripping answers very well where economy is an object. Pieces of underdone roast or boiled meat may in pies be used very advantageously; but always remove the bone from pie-meat, unless it be chicken or game. We have directed that the meat shall be cut smaller than is usually the case; for on trial we have found it much more tender, more easily helped, and with more gravy, than when put into the dish in one or two large steaks.

BEEF-STEAK PIE.

BEEF-STEAKS WITH FRIED POTATOES, or BIFTEK AUX POMMES-DE-TERRE

(à la mode Française)

Ingredients.—2 lbs. of steak, 8 potatoes, ¼ lb. of butter, salt and pepper to taste, 1 teaspoonful of minced herbs.

Mode.—Put the butter into a frying or *sauté* pan, set it over the fire, and let it get very hot; peel, and cut the potatoes into long thin slices; put them into the hot butter, and fry them till of a nice brown colour. Now broil the steaks over a bright clear fire, turning them frequently, that every part may be equally done: as they should not be thick, 5 minutes will broil them. Put the herbs and seasoning in the butter the potatoes were fried in, pour it under the steak, and place the fried potatoes round, as a garnish. To have this dish in perfection, a portion of the fillet of the sirloin should be used, as the meat is generally so much more tender than that of the rump, and the steaks should be cut about ½ inch in thickness.

Time.—5 minutes to broil the steaks, and about the same time to fry the potatoes.

Average cost.—1s. per lb.

Sufficient for 4 persons.

Seasonable all the year; but not so good in warm weather, as the meat cannot hang to get tender.

BUBBLE-AND-SQUEAK

(Cold Meat Cookery)

Ingredients.—A few thin slices of cold boiled beef, butter, cabbage, 1 sliced onion, pepper and salt to taste.

Mode.—Fry the slices of beef gently in a little butter, taking care not to dry them up. Lay them on a flat dish, and cover with fried greens. The greens may be prepared from cabbage sprouts or green savoys. They should be boiled till tender, well drained, minced, and placed, till quite hot, in a frying-pan, with butter, a sliced onion, and seasoning of pepper and salt. When the onion is done, it is ready to serve.

Time.—Altogether, ½ hour.

Average cost, exclusive of the cold beef, 3d.

Seasonable at any time.

BEEF-COLLOPS

Ingredients.—2 lbs. of rump-steak, ¼ lb. of butter, 1 pint of gravy (water may be substituted for this), salt and pepper to taste, 1 shalot finely minced, ½ pickled walnut, 1 teaspoonful of capers.

Mode.—Have the steak cut thin, and divide it in pieces about 3 inches long; beat these with the blade of a knife, and dredge with flour. Put them in a frying-pan with the butter, and let them fry for about 3 minutes; then lay them in a small stewpan, and pour over them the gravy. Add a piece of butter, kneaded with a little flour, put in the seasoning and all the other ingredients, and let the whole simmer, but not boil, for 10 minutes. Serve in a hot covered dish.

Time.—10 minutes.

Average cost.—1s. per lb.

Sufficient for 4 or 5 persons.

Seasonable at any time.

STEWED OX-TAILS

Ingredients.—2 ox-tails, 1 onion, 3 cloves, 1 blade of mace, 1 teaspoonful of whole black pepper, 1 teaspoonful of allspice, ½ teaspoonful of salt, a small bunch of savoury herbs, thickening of butter and flour, 1 tablespoonful of lemon-juice, 1 tablespoonful of mushroom ketchup.

Mode.—Divide the tails at the joints, wash, and put them into a stewpan with sufficient water to cover them, and set them on the fire; when the water boils, remove the scum and add the onion cut into rings, the spice, seasoning, and herbs. Cover the stewpan closely, and let the tails simmer very gently until tender, which will be in about 2½ hours. Take them out, make a thickening of butter and flour, add it to the gravy, and let it boil for ¼ hour. Strain it through a sieve into a saucepan, put back the tails, add the lemon-juice and ketchup; let the whole just boil up, and serve. Garnish with croûtons or sippets of toasted bread.

Time.—2½ hours to stew the tails.

Average cost.—9d. to 1s. 6d., according to the season.

Sufficient for 8 persons.

Seasonable all the year.

POTTED BEEF

Ingredients.—2 lbs. of lean beef, 1 tablespoonful of water, ¼ lb. of butter, a seasoning to taste of salt, cayenne, pounded mace, and black pepper.

Mode.—Procure a nice piece of lean beef, as free as possible from gristle, skin, &c., and put it into a jar (if at hand, one with a lid) with 1 tablespoonful of water. Cover it *closely*, and put the jar into a saucepan of boiling water, letting the water come within 2 inches of the top of the jar. Boil gently for 3½ hours, then take the beef, chop it very small with a chopping-knife, and pound it thoroughly in a mortar. Mix with it by degrees all, or a portion, of the gravy that will have run from it, and a little clarified butter; add the seasoning, put it in small pots for use, and cover with a little butter just warmed and poured over. If much gravy is added to it, it will keep but a short time; on the contrary, if a large proportion of butter is used, it may be preserved for some time.

Time.—3½ hours.

Average cost, for this quantity, 1s. 8d.

Seasonable at any time.

POTTING-JAR.

STEWED SHIN OF BEEF

Ingredients.—A shin of beef, 1 head of celery, 1 onion, a faggot of savoury herbs, ½ teaspoonful of allspice, ½ teaspoonful of whole black pepper, 4 carrots, 12 button onions, 2 turnips, thickening of butter and flour, 3 tablespoonfuls of mushroom ketchup, 2 tablespoonfuls of port wine; pepper and salt to taste.

Mode.—Have the bone sawn into 4 or 5 pieces, cover with hot water, bring it to a boil, and remove any scum that may rise to the surface. Put in the celery, onion, herbs, spice, and seasoning, and simmer very gently until the meat is tender. Peel the vegetables, cut them into any shape fancy may dictate, and boil them with the onions until tender; lift out the beef, put it on a dish, which keep hot, and thicken with butter and flour as much of the liquor as will be wanted for gravy; keep stirring till it boils, then strain and skim. Put the gravy back in the stewpan, add the seasoning, port wine, and ketchup, give one boil, and pour it over the beef; garnish with the boiled carrots, turnips, and onions.

Time.—The meat to be stewed about 4 hours.

Average cost.—4d. per lb. with bone.

Sufficient for 7 or 8 persons.

Seasonable at any time.

BOILED TONGUE

Ingredients.—1 tongue, a bunch of savoury herbs, water.

Mode.—In choosing a tongue, ascertain how long it has been dried or pickled, and select one with a smooth skin, which denotes its being young and tender. If a dried one, and rather hard, soak it at least for 12 hours previous to cooking it; if, however, it is fresh from the pickle, 2 or 3 hours will be sufficient for it to remain in sock. Put the tongue in a stewpan with plenty of cold water and a bunch of savoury herbs; let it gradually come to a boil, skim well and simmer very gently until tender. Peel off the skin, garnish with tufts of cauliflowers or Brussels sprouts, and serve. Boiled tongue is frequently sent to table with boiled poultry, instead of ham, and is, by many persons, preferred. If to serve cold, peel it, fasten it down to a piece of board by sticking a fork through the root, and another through the top, to straighten it. When cold, glaze it, and put a paper ruche round the root, and garnish with tufts of parsley.

Time.—A large smoked tongue, 4 to 4½ hours; a small one, 2½ to 3 hours. A large unsmoked tongue, 3 to 3½ hours; a small one, 2 to 2½ hours.

Average cost, for a moderate-sized tongue, 3s. 6d.

Seasonable at any time.

CHAPTER FIVE

RECIPES FOR COOKING MUTTON AND LAMB

CURRIED MUTTON

(Cold Meat Cookery)

Ingredients.—The remains of any joint of cold mutton, 2 onions, ¼ lb. of butter, 1 dessertspoonful of curry powder, 1 dessertspoonful of flour, salt to taste, ¼ pint of stock or water.

Mode.—Slice the onions in thin rings, and put them into a stewpan with the butter, and fry of a light brown; stir in the curry powder, flour, and salt, and mix all well together. Cut the meat into nice thin slices (if there is not sufficient to do this, it may be minced), and add it to the other ingredients; when well browned, add the stock or gravy, and stew gently for about ½ hour. Serve in a dish with a border of boiled rice, the same as for other curries.

Time.—½ hour.

Average cost, exclusive of the meat, 6d.

Seasonable in winter.

DORMERS

Ingredients.—½ lb. of cold mutton, 2 oz. of beef suet, pepper and salt to taste, 3 oz. of boiled rice, 1 egg, bread crumbs, made gravy.

Mode.—Chop the meat, suet, and rice finely; mix well together, and add a high seasoning of pepper and salt, and roll into sausages; cover them with egg and bread crumbs, and fry in hot dripping of a nice brown. Serve in a dish with made gravy poured round them, and a little in a tureen.

Time.—½ hour to fry the sausages.

Average cost, exclusive of the meat, 6d.

Seasonable at any time.

The Golden Fleece.—The ancient fable of the Golden Fleece may be thus briefly told:—Phryxus, a son of Athamus, king of Thebes, to escape the persecutions of his stepmother Ino, paid a visit to his friend Aeetes, king of Colchis. A ram, whose fleece was of pure gold, carried the youth through the air in a most obliging manner to the court of his friend. When safe at Colchis, Phryxus offered the ram on the altars of Mars, and pocketed the fleece. The king received him with great kindness, and gave him his daughter Chalciope in marriage; but, some time after, he murdered him in order to obtain possession of the precious fleece. The murder of Phryxus was amply revenged by the Greeks. It gave rise to the famous Argonautic expedition, undertaken by Jason and fifty of the most celebrated heroes of Greece. The Argonauts recovered the fleece by the help of the celebrated sorceress Medea, daughter of Aeetes, who fell desperately in love with the gallant but faithless Jason. In the story of the voyage of the Argo, a substratum of truth probably exists, though overlaid by a mass of fiction. The ram which carried Phryxus to Colchis is by some supposed to have been the name of the ship in which he embarked. The fleece of gold is thought to represent the immense treasures he bore away from Thebes. The alchemists of the fifteenth century were firmly convinced that the Golden Fleece was a treatise on the transmutation of metals, written on sheepskin.

IRISH STEW

Ingredients.—3 lbs. of the loin or neck of mutton, 5 lbs. of potatoes, 5 large onions, pepper and salt to taste, rather more than 1 pint of water.

Mode.—Trim off some of the fat of the above quantity of loin or neck of mutton, and cut it into chops of a moderate thickness. Pare and halve the potatoes, and cut the onions into thick slices. Put a layer of potatoes at the bottom of a stewpan, then a layer of mutton and onions, and season with pepper and salt; proceed in this manner until the stewpan is full, taking care to have plenty of vegetables at the top. Pour in the water, and let it stew very gently for 2½ hours, keeping the lid of the stewpan closely shut the *whole* time, and occasionally shaking it to prevent its burning.

Time.—2½ hours.

Average cost, for this quantity, 2s. 8d.

Sufficient for 5 or 6 persons.

Seasonable.—More suitable for a winter dish.

ROAST SADDLE OF MUTTON

Ingredients.—Saddle of mutton, a little salt.

Mode.—To insure this joint being tender, let it hang for ten days or a fortnight, if the weather permits. Cut off the tail and flaps and trim away every part that has not indisputable pretensions to be eaten, and have the skin taken off and skewered on again. Put it down to a bright clear fire, and, when the joint has been cooking for an hour, remove the skin and dredge it with flour. It should not be placed too near the fire, as the fat should not be in the slightest degree burnt. Keep constantly basting, both before and after the skin is removed; sprinkle some salt over the joint. Make a little gravy in the dripping-pan; pour it over the meat, which send to table with a tureen of made gravy and red-currant jelly.

Time.—A saddle of mutton weighing 10 lbs., 2½ hours; 14 lbs., 3¼ hours. When liked underdone, allow rather less time.

Average cost.—10d. per lb.

Sufficient.—A moderate-sized saddle of 10 lbs. for 7 or 8 persons.

Seasonable all the year; not so good when lamb is in full season.

SADDLE OF MUTTON.

SHEEP'S BRAINS, EN MATELOTE

(An Entrée)

Ingredients.—6 sheep's brains, vinegar, salt, a few slices of bacon, 1 small onion, 2 cloves, a small bunch of parsley, sufficient stock or weak broth to cover the brains, 1 tablespoonful of lemon-juice, matelote sauce.

Mode.—Detach the brains from the heads without breaking them, and put them into a pan of warm water; remove the skin, and let them remain for 2 hours. Have ready a saucepan of boiling water, add a little vinegar and salt, and put in the brains. When they are quite firm, take them out and put them into very cold water. Place 2 or 3 slices of bacon in a stewpan, put in the brains, the onion stuck with 2 cloves, the parsley, and a good seasoning of pepper and salt; cover with stock, or weak broth, and boil them gently for about 25 minutes. Have ready some croûtons; arrange these in the dish alternately with the brains, and cover with a matelote sauce, to which has been added the above proportion of lemon-juice.

Time.—25 minutes.

Average cost.—1s. 6d.

Sufficient for 6 persons.

Seasonable at any time.

SHEEP'S FEET or TROTTERS

(Soyer's Recipe)

Ingredients.—12 feet, ¼ lb. of beef or mutton suet, 2 onions, 1 carrot, 2 bay-leaves, 2 sprigs of thyme, 1 oz. of salt, ¼ oz. of pepper, 2 tablespoonfuls of flour, 2½ quarts of water, ¼ lb. of fresh butter, 1 teaspoonful of salt, 1 teaspoonful of flour, ¾ teaspoonful of pepper, a little grated nutmeg, the juice of 1 lemon, 1 gill of milk, the yolks of 2 eggs.

Mode.—Have the feet cleaned, and the long bone extracted from them. Put the suet into a stewpan, with the onions and carrot sliced, the bay-leaves, thyme, salt, and pepper, and let these simmer for 5 minutes. Add 2 tablespoonfuls of flour and the water, and keep stirring till it boils; then put in the feet. Let these simmer for 3 hours, or until perfectly tender, and take them and lay them on a sieve. Mix together, on a plate, with the back of a spoon, butter, salt, flour (1 teaspoonful), pepper, nutmeg, and lemon-juice as above, and put the feet, with a gill of milk, into a stewpan. When very hot, add the butter, &c., and stir continually till melted. Now mix the yolks of 2 eggs with 5 tablespoonfuls of milk; stir this to the other ingredients, keep moving the pan over the fire continually for a minute or two, but do not allow it to boil after the eggs are added. Serve in a very hot dish, and garnish with croûtons, or sippets of toasted bread.

Time.—3 hours.

Average cost.—1s. 6d.

Sufficient for 4 persons.

Seasonable at any time.

TO DRESS A SHEEP'S HEAD

Ingredients.—1 sheep's head, sufficient water to cover it, 3 carrots, 3 turnips, 2 or 3 parsnips, 3 onions, a small bunch of parsley, 1 teaspoonful of pepper, 3 teaspoonfuls of salt, ¼ lb. of Scotch oatmeal.

Mode.—Clean the head well, and let it soak in warm water for 2 hours, to get rid of the blood; put it into a saucepan, with sufficient cold water to cover it, and when it boils, add the vegetables, peeled and sliced, and the remaining ingredients; before adding the oatmeal, mix it to a smooth batter with a little of the liquor. Keep stirring till it boils up; then shut the saucepan closely, and let it stew gently for 1½ or 2 hours. It may be thickened with rice or barley, but oatmeal is preferable.

Time.—1½ or 2 hours.

Average cost.—8d. each.

Sufficient for 3 persons.

Seasonable at any time.

Singed Sheep's Head.—The village of Dudingston, which stands "within a mile of Edinburgh town," was formerly celebrated for this ancient and homely Scottish dish. In the summer months, many opulent citizens used to resort to this place to solace themselves over singed sheep's heads, boiled or baked. The sheep fed upon the neighbouring hills were slaughtered at this village, and the carcases were sent to town; but the heads were left to be consumed in the place. We are not aware whether the custom of eating sheep's heads at Dudingston is still kept up by the good folks of Edinburgh.

ROAST LEG OF LAMB

Ingredients.—Lamb, a little salt.

Mode.—Place the joint at a good distance from the fire at first, and baste well the whole time it is cooking. When nearly done, draw it nearer the fire to acquire a nice brown colour. Sprinkle a little fine salt over the meat, empty the dripping-pan of its contents; pour in a little boiling water, and strain this over the meat. Serve with mint sauce and a fresh salad, and for vegetables send peas, spinach, or cauliflowers to table with it.

Time.—A leg of lamb weighing 5 lbs., 1½ hour.

Average cost.—10d to 1s. per lb.

Sufficient for 4 or 5 persons.

Seasonable from Easter to Michaelmas.

LEG OF LAMB.

BRAISED LOIN OF LAMB

Ingredients.—1 loin of lamb, a few slices of bacon, 1 bunch of green onions, 5 or 6 young carrots, a bunch of savoury herbs, 2 blades of pounded mace, 1 pint of stock, salt to taste.

Mode.—Bone a loin of lamb, and line the bottom of a stewpan just capable of holding it, with a few thin slices of fat bacon; add the remaining ingredients, cover the meat with a few more slices of bacon, pour in the stock, and simmer very *gently* for 2 hours; take it up, dry it, strain and reduce the gravy to a glaze, with which glaze the meat, and serve it either on stewed peas, spinach, or stewed cucumbers.

Time.—2 hours.

Average cost.—11d. per lb.

Sufficient for 4 or 5 persons.

Seasonable from Easter to Michaelmas.

LOIN OF LAMB.

ROAST SADDLE OF LAMB

Ingredients.—Lamb, a little salt.

Mode.—This joint is now very much in vogue, and is generally considered a nice one for a small party. Have ready a clear brisk fire; put down the joint at a little distance, to prevent the fat from scorching, and keep it well basted all the time it is cooking. Serve with mint sauce and a fresh salad, and send to table with it, either peas, cauliflowers, or spinach.

Time.—A small saddle, 1½ hour; a large one, 2 hours.

Average cost.—10d. to 1s. per lb.

Sufficient for 5 or 6 persons.

Seasonable from Easter to Michaelmas.

Note.—Loin and ribs of lamb are roasted in the same manner, and served with the same sauces as the above. A loin will take about 1¼ hour; ribs, from 1 to 1¼ hour.

SADDLE OF LAMB.

RIBS OF LAMB.

CHAPTER SIX

RECIPES FOR COOKING PORK

PORK CUTLETS

(Cold Meat Cookery)

Ingredients.—The remains of cold roast loin of pork, 1 oz. of butter, 2 onions, 1 dessertspoonful of flour, ½ pint of gravy, pepper and salt to taste, 1 teaspoonful of vinegar and mustard.

Mode.—Cut the pork into nice-sized cutlets, trim off most of the fat, and chop the onions. Put the butter into a stewpan, lay in the cutlets and chopped onions, and fry a light brown; then add the remaining ingredients, simmer gently for 5 or 7 minutes, and serve.

Time.—5 to 7 minutes.

Average cost, exclusive of the meat, 4d.

Seasonable from October to March.

ROAST LEG OF PORK

Ingredients.—Leg of pork, a little oil for stuffing.

Mode.—Choose a small leg of pork, and score the skin across in narrow strips, about ¼ inch apart. Cut a slit in the knuckle, loosen the skin, and fill it with a sage-and-onion stuffing. Brush the joint over with a little salad-oil (this makes the crackling crisper, and a better colour), and put it down to a bright, clear fire, not too near, as that would cause the skin to blister. Baste it well, and serve with a little gravy made in the dripping-pan, and do not omit to send to table with it a tureen of well-made apple-sauce.

Time.—A leg of pork weighing 8 lbs., about 3 hours.

Average cost.—9d. per lb.

Sufficient for 6 or 7 persons.

Seasonable from September to March.

ROAST LEG OF PORK.

TO BAKE A HAM

Ingredients.—Ham; a common crust.

Mode.—As a ham for baking should be well soaked, let it remain in water for at least 12 hours. Wipe it dry, trim away any rusty places underneath, and cover it with a common crust, taking care that this is of sufficient thickness all over to keep the gravy in. Place it in a moderately-heated oven, and bake for nearly 4 hours. Take off the crust, and skin, and cover with raspings, the same as for boiled ham, and garnish the knuckle with a paper frill. This method of cooking a ham is, by many persons, considered far superior to boiling it, as it cuts fuller of gravy and has a finer flavour, besides keeping a much longer time good.

Time.—A medium-sized ham, 4 hours.

Average cost.—from 8d. to 10d. per lb. by the whole ham.

Seasonable all the year.

FRIED HAM AND EGGS

(A Breakfast Dish)

Ingredients.—Ham, eggs.

Mode.—Cut the ham into slices, and take care that they are of the same thickness in every part. Cut off the rind, and if the ham should be particularly hard and salty, it will be found an improvement to soak it for about 10 minutes in hot water, and then dry it in a cloth. Put it into a cold frying-pan, set it over the fire, and turn the slices 3 or 4 times whilst they are cooking. When done, place them on a dish, which should be kept hot in front of the fire during the time the eggs are being poached. Poach the eggs, slip them on to the slices of ham, and serve quickly.

Time.—7 or 8 minutes to broil the ham.

Average cost.—from 8d. to 10d. per lb. by the whole ham.

Seasonable at any time.

Note.—Ham may also be toasted or broiled; but, with the latter method, to insure its being well cooked, the fire must be beautifully clear, or it will have a smoky flavour far from agreeable.

COLLARED PIG'S FACE

(A Breakfast or Luncheon Dish)

Ingredients.—1 pig's face, salt. For brine, 1 gallon of spring water, 1 lb. of common salt, ½ handful of chopped juniper-berries, 6 bruised cloves, 2 bay-leaves, a few sprigs of thyme, basil, sage, ¼ oz. of saltpetre. For forcemeat, ½ lb. of ham, ½ lb. bacon, 1 teaspoonful of mixed spices, pepper to taste, ¼ lb. of lard, 1 tablespoonful of minced parsley, 6 young onions.

PIG'S FACE.

Mode.—Singe the head carefully, bone it without breaking the skin, and rub it well with salt. Make the brine by boiling the above ingredients for ¼ hour, and letting it stand to cool. When cold, pour it over the head, and let it steep in this for 10 days, turning and rubbing it often. Then wipe, drain, and dry it. For the forcemeat, pound the ham and bacon very finely, and mix with these the remaining ingredients, taking care that the whole is thoroughly incorporated. Spread this equally over the head, roll it tightly in a cloth, and bind it securely with broad tape. Put it into a saucepan with a few meat trimmings, and cover it with stock; let it simmer gently for 4 hours, and be particular that it does not stop boiling the whole time. When quite tender, take it up, put it between 2 dishes with a heavy weight on the top, and when cold, remove the cloth and tape. It should be sent to table on a napkin, or garnished with a piece of deep white paper with a ruche at the top.

Time.—4 hours.

Average cost.—from 2s. to 2s. 6d.

Seasonable from October to March.

The Wild and Domestic Hog.—The domestic hog is the descendant of a race long since banished from this island; and it is remarkable, that while the tamed animal has been and is kept under surveillance, the wild type whence this race sprung, has maintained itself in its ancient freedom, the fierce denizen of the forest, and one of the renowned beasts of the chase. Whatever doubt may exist as to the true origin of the dog, the horse, the ox, and others, or as to whether their original race is yet extant or not, these doubts do not apply to the domestic hog. Its wild source still exists, and is universally recognised: like the wolf, however, it has been expelled from our island; but, like that animal, it still roams through the vast wooded tracts of Europe and Asia.

BOILED LEG OF PORK

Ingredients.—Leg of pork, salt.

Mode.—For boiling, choose a small, compact, well-filled leg, and rub it well with salt; let it remain in pickle for a week or 10 days, turning and rubbing it every day. An hour before dressing it, put it into cold water for an hour, which improves the colour. If the pork is purchased ready salted, ascertain how long the meat has been in pickle, and soak it accordingly. Put it into a boiling-pot, with sufficient cold water to cover it; let it gradually come to a boil, and remove the scum as it rises. Simmer it very gently until tender, and do not allow it to boil fast, or the knuckle will fall to pieces before the middle of the leg is done. Carrots, turnips, or parsnips may be boiled with the pork, some of which should be laid round the dish as a garnish, and a well-made pease-pudding is an indispensable accompaniment.

Time.—A leg of pork weighing 8 lbs., 3 hours after the water boils, and to be simmered very gently.

Average cost.—9d. per lb.

Sufficient for 7 or 8 persons.

Seasonable from September to March.

Note.—The liquor in which a leg of pork has been boiled, makes excellent pea-soup.

Antiquity of the Hog.—The hog has survived changes which have swept multitudes of pachydermatous animals from the surface of our earth. It still presents the same characteristics, both physical and moral, which the earliest writers, whether sacred or profane, have faithfully delineated. Although the domestic has been more or less modified by long culture, yet the wild species remains unaltered, insomuch that the fossil relics may be identified with the bones of their existing descendants.

LARDING

Ingredients.—Bacon and larding-needle.

Mode.—Bacon for larding should be firm and fat, and ought to be cured without any saltpetre, as this reddens white meats. Lay it on a table, the rinds downwards; trim off any rusty part, and cut it into slices of an equal thickness. Place the slices one on the top of another and cut them evenly into narrow strips, so arranging it that every piece of bacon is of the same size. Bacon for fricandeau, poultry, and game, should be about 2 inches in length, and rather more than one-eighth of an inch in width. If for larding fillets of beef or loin of veal, the pieces of bacon must be thicker. The following recipe of Soyer is, we think, very explicit; and any cook, by following the directions here given, may be able to lard, if not well, sufficiently for general use.

"Have the fricandeau trimmed, lay it, lengthwise, upon a clean napkin across your hand, forming a kind of bridge with your thumb at the part you are about to commence at; then with the point of the larding-needle make three distinct lines across, ½ inch apart; run the needle into the third line, at the further side of the fricandeau, and bring it out at the first, placing one of the lardoons in it; draw the needle through, leaving out ¼ inch of the bacon at each line; proceed thus to the end of the row; then make another line, ½ inch distant, stick in another row of lardoons, bringing them out at the second line, leaving the ends of the bacon out all the same length; make the next row again at the same distance, bringing the ends out between the lardoons of the first row, proceeding in this manner until the whole surface is larded in chequered rows. Everything else is larded in a similar way; and, in the case of poultry, hold the breast over a charcoal fire for one minute, or dip it into boiling water, in order to make the flesh firm."

BACON FOR LARDING, AND
LARDING-NEEDLE.

LITTLE RAISED PORK PIES

Ingredients.—2 lbs. of flour, ½ lb. of butter, ½ lb. of mutton suet, salt and white pepper to taste, 4 lbs. of the neck of pork, 1 dessertspoonful of powdered sage.

Mode.—Well dry the flour, mince the suet, and put these with the butter into a saucepan, to be made hot, and add a little salt. When melted, mix it up into a stiff paste, and put it before the fire with a cloth over it until ready to make up; chop the pork into small pieces, season it with white pepper, salt, and powdered sage; divide the paste into rather small pieces, raise it in a round or oval form, fill with the meat, and bake in a brick oven. These pies will require a fiercer oven than normal-sized pork pies as they are made so much smaller, and consequently do not require so soaking a heat.

Time.—If made small, about 1½ hour.

Seasonable from September to March.

Swineherds of Antiquity.—From the prejudice against the hog among the ancients, those who tended them formed an isolated class, and were esteemed as the outcasts of society. However much the flesh of the animal was esteemed by the Greeks and Romans, yet the swineherd is not mentioned by either the classic writers or the poets who, in ancient Greece and Rome, painted rural life. We have no descriptions of gods or heroes descending to the occupation of keeping swine. The swineherd is never introduced into the idyls of Theocritus, nor has Virgil admitted him into his eclogues. The Eumaeus of Homer is the only exception that we have of a swineherd meeting with favour in the eyes of a poet of antiquity. This may be accounted for, on the supposition that the prejudices of the Egyptians relative to this class of men, extended to both Greece and Italy, and imparted a bias to popular opinion.

ROAST SUCKING-PIG

Ingredients.—Pig, 6 oz. of bread crumbs, 16 sage-leaves, pepper and salt to taste, a piece of butter the size of an egg, salad-oil or butter to baste with, about ½ pint of gravy, 1 tablespoonful of lemon-juice.

Mode.—A sucking-pig, to be eaten in perfection, should not be more than three weeks old, and should be dressed the same day that it is killed. After preparing the pig for cooking, as in the preceding recipe, stuff it with finely-grated bread crumbs, minced sage, pepper, salt, and a piece of butter the size of an egg, all of which should be well mixed together, and put into the body of the pig. Sew up the slit neatly, and truss the legs back, to allow the inside to be roasted, and the under part to be crisp. Put the pig down to a bright clear fire, not too near, and let it lay till thoroughly dry; then have ready some butter tied up in a piece of thin cloth, and rub the pig with this in every part. Keep it well rubbed with the butter the whole of the time it is roasting, and do not allow the crackling to become blistered or burnt. When half-done, hang a pig-iron before the middle part (if this is not obtainable, use a flat iron), to prevent its being scorched and dried up before the ends are done. Before it is taken from the fire, cut off the head, and part that and the body down the middle. Chop the brains and mix them with the stuffing; add ½ pint of good gravy, a tablespoonful of lemon-juice, and the gravy that flowed from the pig; put a little of this on the dish with the pig, and the remainder send to table in a tureen. Place the pig back to back in the dish, with one half of the head on each side, and one of the ears at each end, and send it to table as hot as possible. Instead of butter, many cooks take salad-oil for basting, which makes the crackling crisp; and as this is one of the principal things to be considered, perhaps it is desirable to use it; but be particular that it is very pure, or it will impart an unpleasant flavour to the meat. The brains and stuffing may be stirred into a tureen of melted butter instead of gravy, when the latter is not liked. Apple sauce and the old-fashioned currant sauce are not yet quite obsolete as an accompaniment to roast pig.

Time.—1½ to 2 hours for a small pig.

Average cost.—5s. to 6s.

Sufficient for 9 or 10 persons.

Seasonable from September to February.

CHAPTER SEVEN

RECIPES FOR COOKING POULTRY

CHICKEN OR FOWL PIE

Ingredients.—2 small fowls or 1 large one, white pepper and salt to taste, ½ teaspoonful of grated nutmeg, ½ teaspoonful of pounded mace, forcemeat, a few slices of ham, 3 hard-boiled eggs, ½ pint of water, puff crust.

Mode.—Skin and cut up the fowls into joints, and put the neck, legs and backbones in a stewpan, with a little water, an onion, a bunch of savoury herbs, and a blade of mace; let these stew for about an hour, and, when done, strain off the liquor: this is for gravy. Put a layer of fowl at the bottom of a pie-dish, then a layer of ham, then one of forcemeat and hard-boiled eggs cut in rings; between the layers put a seasoning of pounded mace, nutmeg, pepper, and salt. Proceed in this manner until the dish is full, and pour in about ½ pint of water; border the edge of the dish with puff crust, put on the cover, ornament the top, and glaze it by brushing over it the yolk of an egg. Bake from 1¼ to 1½ hour, should the pie be very large, and, when done, pour in, at the top, the gravy made from the bones. If to be eaten cold, and wished particularly nice, the joints of the fowls should be boned, and placed in the dish with alternate layers of forcemeat; sausage-meat may also be substituted for the forcemeat, and is now very much used. When the chickens are boned, and mixed with sausage-meat, the pie will take about 2 hours to bake. It should be covered with a piece of paper when about half-done, to prevent the paste from being dried up or scorched.

Time.—For a pie with unboned meat, 1¼ to 1½ hour; with boned meat and sausage or forcemeat, 1½ to 2 hours.

Average cost, with 2 fowls, 6s. 6d.

Sufficient for 6 or 7 persons.

Seasonable at any time.

The Young Chicks.—The chicks that are hatched first should be taken from underneath the hen, lest she might think her task at an end, and leave the remaining eggs to spoil. As soon as the young birds are taken from the mother, they must be placed in a basket lined with soft wool, flannel, or hay, and stood in the sunlight if it be summer time, or by the fire if the weather be cold. It is a common practice to cram young chicks with food as soon as they are born. This is quite unnecessary. They will, so long as they are kept warm, come to no harm if they take no food for twenty-four hours following their birth. Should the whole of the brood not be hatched by that time, those that are born may be fed with bread soaked in milk, and the yolk of a hard-boiled egg.

POTTED CHICKEN OR FOWL
(A Luncheon or Breakfast Dish)

Ingredients.—The remains of cold roast chicken; to every lb. of meat allow ¼ lb. of fresh butter, salt and cayenne to taste, 1 teaspoonful of pounded mace, ¼ small nutmeg.

Mode.—Strip the meat from the bones of cold roast fowl; when it is freed from gristle and skin, weigh it, and, to every lb. of meat, allow the above proportion of butter, seasoning, and spices. Cut the meat into small pieces, pound it well with the fresh butter, sprinkle in the spices gradually, and keep pounding until reduced to a perfectly smooth paste. Put it into potting-pots for use, and cover it with clarified butter, about ¼ inch in thickness, and, if to be kept for some time, tie over a bladder: 2 or 3 slices of ham, minced and pounded with the above ingredients, will be found an improvement. It should be kept in a dry place.

Seasonable at any time.

Feeding and Cooping the Chicks.—When all the chicks are hatched, they should be placed along with the mother under a coop in a warm dry spot. If two hens happen to have their broods at the same time, their respective chicks should be carefully kept separate; as, if they get mixed, and so go under the wrong coop, the hens will probably maim and destroy those who have mistaken their dwelling. After being kept snug beneath the coop for a week (the coop should be placed under cover at nightfall), the chicks may be turned loose for an hour or so in the warmest part of the day. They should be gradually weaned from the soaked bread and chopped egg, instead of which grits or boiled barley should be given; in 8 or 10 days their stomachs will be strong enough to receive bruised barley, and at the end of 3 weeks, if your chicks be healthy, they will be able to take care of themselves. It will be well, however, to keep your eye on them a week or so longer, as the elder chickens may drive them from their food. Great care should be taken that the very young chicks do not run about the wet ground or on damp grass, as this is the most prominent and fatal cause of disease. While under the coop with their mother, a shallow pan or plate of water should be supplied to the chicks, as in a deeper vessel they are liable to drench themselves and take cold, or possibly to get drowned.

ROAST DUCKS

Ingredients.—A couple of ducks, sage-and-onion stuffing, a little flour.

Choosing and Trussing.—Choose ducks with plump bellies, and with thick and yellowish feet. They should be trussed with the feet on, which should be scalded, and the skin peeled off, and then turned up close to the legs. Run a skewer through the middle of each leg, after having drawn them as close as possible to the body, to plump up the breast, passing the same quite through the body. Cut off the heads and necks, and the pinions at the first joint; bring these close to the sides, twist the feet round, and truss them at the back of the bird. After the duck is stuffed, both ends should be secured with string, so as to keep in the seasoning.

ROAST DUCK.

Mode.—To insure ducks being tender, never dress them the same day they are killed; and if the weather permits, they should hang a day or two. Make a stuffing of sage and onion sufficient for one duck, and leave the other unseasoned, as the flavour is not liked by everybody. Put them down to a brisk clear

113

fire, and keep them well basted the whole of the time they are cooking. A few minutes before serving, dredge them lightly with flour, to make them froth and look plump; and when the steam draws towards the fire, send them to table hot and quickly, with a good brown gravy poured *round*, but not *over* the ducks, and a little of the same in a tureen. When in season, green peas should invariably accompany this dish.

Time.—Full-grown ducks from ¾ to 1 hour; ducklings from 25 to 35 minutes.

Average cost.—from 2s. 3d. to 2s. 6d. each.

Sufficient.—A couple of ducks for 6 or 7 persons.

Seasonable.—Ducklings from April to August; ducks from November to February.

Note.—Ducklings are trussed and roasted in the same manner, and served with the same sauces and accompaniments. When in season, serve apple sauce.

STEWED DUCK AND PEAS

(Cold Meat Cookery)

Ingredients.—The remains of cold roast duck, 2 oz. of butter, 3 or 4 slices of lean ham or bacon, 1 tablespoonful of flour, 2 pints of thin gravy, 1, or a small bunch of green onions, 3 sprigs of parsley, 3 cloves, 1 pint of young green peas, cayenne and salt to taste, 1 teaspoonful of pounded sugar.

Mode.—Put the butter into a stewpan; cut up the duck into joints, lay them in with the slices of lean ham or bacon; make it brown, then dredge in a tablespoonful of flour, and stir this well in before adding the gravy. Put in the onion, parsley, cloves, and gravy, and when it has simmered for ¼ hour, add a pint of young green peas, and stew gently for about ½ hour. Season with cayenne, salt, and sugar; take out the duck, place it round the dish, and the peas in the middle.

Time.—¾ hour.

Average cost, exclusive of the cold duck, 1s.

Seasonable from June to August.

Ducks Hatching.—Concerning incubation by ducks, a practised writer says, "The duck requires a secret and safe place, rather than any attendance, and will, at nature's call, cover her eggs and seek her food. On hatching, there is not often a necessity for taking away any of the brood; and, having hatched, let the mother retain her young ones upon the nest her own time. On her moving with her brood, let a coop be prepared upon the short grass, if the weather be fine, and under shelter, if otherwise."

Cooping and Feeding Ducklings.—Brood ducks should be cooped at some distance from any other. A wide and flat dish of water, to be often renewed, should stand just outside the coop, and barley, or any other meal, be the first food of the ducklings. It will be needful, if it be wet weather, to clip their tails, lest these draggle, and so weaken the bird. The period of the duck's confinement to the coop will depend on the weather, and on the strength of the ducklings. A fortnight is usually the extent of time necessary, and they may even be sometimes permitted to enjoy the luxury of a swim at the end of a week. They should not, however, be allowed to stay too long in the water at first; for they will then become ill, their feathers get rough, and looseness of the bowels ensue. In the latter case, let them be closely cooped for a few days, and bean-meal or oatmeal be mixed with their ordinary food.

AYLESBURY DUCKS.

BOILED FOWL AND RICE

Ingredients.—1 fowl, mutton broth, 2 onions, 2 small blades of pounded mace, pepper and salt to taste, ¼ pint of rice, parsley and butter.

Mode.—Truss the fowl as for boiling, and put it into a stewpan with sufficient clear well-skimmed mutton broth to cover it; add the onion, mace, and a seasoning of pepper and salt; stew very gently for about 1 hour, should the fowl be large, and about ½ hour before it is ready put in the rice, which should be well washed and soaked. When the latter is tender, strain it from the liquor, and put it on a sieve reversed to dry before the fire, and, in the mean time, keep the fowl hot. Dish it, put the rice round as a border, pour a little parsley and butter over the fowl, and the remainder send to table in a tureen.

Time.—A large fowl, 1 hour.

Average cost, in full season, 2s. 6d.

Sufficient for 3 or 4 persons.

Seasonable all the year, but scarce in early spring.

The Dorking.—This bird takes its name from that of a town in Surrey, where the breed is to be found in greater numbers, and certainly in greater perfection, than elsewhere. It is generally believed that this particular branch of poultry was found in the town above mentioned as long ago as the Roman era. The Dorking's chief characteristic is that he has five claws on each foot; the extra claw, however, is never of sufficient length to encumber the foot, or to cause it to "drag" its nest, or scratch out the eggs. The colour of the true Dorking is pure white; long in the body, short in the legs, and a prolific layer. Thirty years ago, there was much controversy respecting the origin of the Dorking. The men of Sussex declared that the bird belonged to them, and brought birds indigenous to their weald, and possessing all the Dorking fine points and peculiarities, in proof of the declaration. Others inclined to the belief that the Poland bird was the father of the Dorking, and not without at least a show of reason, as the former bird much resembles the latter in shape; and, despite its sombre hue, it is well known that the Poland cock will occasionally beget thorough white stock from white English hens. The commotion has, however, long ago subsided, and Dorking still retains its fair reputation for fowl.

DORKINGS.

118

GIBLET PIE

Ingredients.—A set of duck or goose giblets, 1 lb. of rump-steak, 1 onion, ½ teaspoonful of whole black pepper, a bunch of savoury herbs, plain crust.

Mode.—Clean, and put the giblets into a stewpan with an onion, whole pepper, and a bunch of savoury herbs; add rather more than a pint of water, and simmer gently for about 1½ hour. Take them out, let them cool, and cut them into pieces; line the bottom of a pie-dish with a few pieces of rump-steak; add a layer of giblets and a few more pieces of steak; season with pepper and salt, and pour in the gravy (which should be strained), that the giblets were stewed in; cover with a plain crust, and bake for rather more than 1½ hour in a brisk oven. Cover a piece of paper over the pie, to prevent the crust taking too much colour.

Time.—1½ hour to stew the giblets, about 1 hour to bake the pie.

Average cost, exclusive of the giblets, 1s. 4d.

Sufficient for 5 or 6 persons.

The Brent Goose.—This is the smallest and most numerous species of the geese which visit the British islands. It makes its appearance in winter, and ranges over the whole of the coasts and estuaries frequented by other migrant geese. Mr. Selby states that a very large body of these birds annually resort to the extensive sandy and muddy flats which lie between the mainland and Holy Island, on the Northumbrian coast, and which are covered by every flow of the tide. This part of the coast appears to have been a favourite resort of these birds from time immemorial, where they have always received the name of Ware geese, no doubt from their continually feeding on marine vegetables. Their flesh is very agreeable.

HASHED GOOSE

Ingredients.—The remains of cold roast goose, 2 onions, 2 oz. of butter, 1 pint of boiling water, 1 dessertspoonful of flour, pepper and salt to taste, 1 tablespoonful of port wine, 2 tablespoonfuls of mushroom ketchup.

Mode.—Cut up the goose into pieces of the size required; the inferior joints, trimmings, &c., put into a stewpan to make the gravy; slice and fry the onions in the butter of a very pale brown; add these to the trimmings, and pour over about a pint of boiling water; stew these gently for ¾ hour, then skim and strain the liquor. Thicken it with flour, and flavour with port wine and ketchup, in the above proportion; add a seasoning of pepper and salt, and put in the pieces of goose; let these get thoroughly hot through, but do not allow them to boil, and serve with sippets of toasted bread.

Time.—Altogether rather more than 1 hour.

Average cost, exclusive of the cold goose, 4d.

Seasonable from September to March.

The Wild Goose.—This bird is sometimes called the "Gray-lag" and is the original of the domestic goose. It is, according to Pennant, the only species which the Britons could take young, and familiarise. "The Gray-lag," says Mr. Gould, "is known to Persia, and we believe it is generally dispersed over Asia Minor." It is the bird that saved the Capitol by its vigilance, and by the Romans was cherished accordingly.

PIGEON PIE

(Epsom Grand-Stand Recipe)

Ingredients.—1½ lb. of rump-steak, 2 or 3 pigeons, 3 slices of ham, pepper and salt to taste, 2 oz. of butter, 4 eggs, puff crust.

Mode.—Cut the steak into pieces about 3 inches square, and with it line the bottom of a pie-dish, seasoning it well with pepper and salt. Clean the pigeons, rub them with pepper and salt inside and out, and put into the body of each rather more than ½ oz. of butter; lay them on the steak, and a piece of ham on each pigeon. Add the yolks of 4 eggs, and half fill the dish with stock; place a border of puff paste round the edge of the dish, put on the cover, and ornament it in any way that may be preferred. Clean three of the feet, and place them in a hole made in the crust at the top: this shows what kind of pie it is. Glaze the crust,—that is to say, brush it over with the yolk of an egg,—and bake it in a well-heated oven for about 1¼ hour. When liked, a seasoning of pounded mace may be added.

Time.—1¼ hour, or rather less.

Average cost.—5s. 3d.

Sufficient for 5 or 6 persons.

Seasonable at any time.

The Tumbler Pigeons.—The smaller the size of this variety, the greater its value. The head should be round and smooth, the neck thin, and the tail similar to that of the turbit. Highly-bred birds of this variety will attain an elevation in their flight beyond that of any other pigeons; and it is in seeing these little birds wing themselves so far into the skies that the fanciers take such delight. For four or five hours tumblers have been known to keep on the wing; and it is when they are almost lost to the power of human vision that they exhibit those pantomimic feats which give them their name, and which are marked by a tumbling over-and-over process, which suggests the idea of their having suddenly become giddy, been deprived of their self-control, or overtaken by some calamity. This acrobatic propensity in these pigeons has been ascribed by some to the absence of a proper power in the tail; but is nothing more than a natural habit, for which no adequate reason can be assigned. Of this variety, the Almond Tumbler is the most beautiful; and the greater the variation of the colour in the flight and tail, the greater their value.

TUMBLER PIGEONS.

The Wood, or Wild Pigeon.—Buffon enumerates upwards of thirty varieties of the pigeon, which he derives from one root,—viz. the stockdove, or common wild pigeon. All the varieties of colour and form which we witness, he attributes to human contrivance and fancy. Nevertheless, there exist essentially specific differences in these birds, which would appear to be attributable rather to the nature of the region, soil, and climate to which they are indigenous, than to the art and ingenuity of man. The stockdove, in its wild state, is still found in some parts of Britain, forming its nest in the holes of rocks, old towers, and in the hollows of trees; it never, however, like the ringdove, nestles in the branches. Multitudes of wild pigeons still visit our shores in the winter, coming from their more northerly retreats, making their appearance about November, and retiring again in the spring. When forests of beechwood covered large tracts of the ground of this country, these birds used to haunt them in myriads, frequently covering a mile of ground in extent when they went out in the morning to feed.

WOOD-PIGEON.

RABBIT PIE

Ingredients.—1 rabbit, a few slices of ham, salt and white pepper to taste, 2 blades of pounded mace, ½ teaspoonful of grated nutmeg, a few forcemeat balls, 3 hard-boiled eggs, ½ pint of gravy, puff crust.

Mode.—Cut up the rabbit (which should be young), remove the breast-bone, and bone the legs. Put the rabbit, slices of ham, forcemeat balls, and hard eggs, by turns, in layers, and season each layer with pepper, salt, pounded mace, and grated nutmeg. Pour in about ½ pint of water, cover with crust, and bake in a well-heated oven for about 1½ hour. Should the crust acquire too much colour, place a piece of paper over it to prevent its burning. When done, pour in at the top, by means of the hole in the middle of the crust, a little good gravy, which may be made of the breast- and leg-bones of the rabbit and 2 or 3 shank-bones, flavoured with onion, herbs, and spices.

Time.—1½ hour.

Average cost.—from 1s. to 1s. 6d. each.

Sufficient for 5 or 6 persons.

Seasonable from September to February.

Note.—The liver of the rabbit may be boiled, minced, and mixed with the forcemeat balls, when the flavour is liked.

Fecundity of the Rabbit.—The fruitfulness of this animal has been the subject of wonder to all naturalists. It breeds seven times in the year, and generally begets seven or eight young ones at a time. If we suppose this to happen regularly for a period of four years, the progeny that would spring from a single pair would amount to more than a million. As the rabbit, however, has many enemies, it can never be permitted to increase in numbers to such an extent as to prove injurious to mankind; for it not only furnishes man with an article of food, but is, by carnivorous animals of every description, mercilessly sacrificed. Notwithstanding this, however, in the time of the Roman power, they once infested the Balearic islands to such an extent, that the inhabitants were obliged to implore the assistance of a military force from Augustus to exterminate them.

STEWED RABBIT, Larded

Ingredients.—1 rabbit, a few strips of bacon, rather more than 1 pint of good broth or stock, a bunch of savoury herbs, salt and pepper to taste, thickening of butter and flour, 1 glass of sherry.

Mode.—Well wash the rabbit, cut it into quarters, lard them with strips of bacon, and fry them; then put them into a stewpan with the broth, herbs, and a seasoning of pepper and salt; simmer gently until the rabbit is tender, then strain the gravy, thicken it with butter and flour, add the sherry, give one boil, pour it over the rabbit, and serve. Garnish with slices of cut lemon.

Time.—Rather more than ½ hour.

Average cost.—1s. to 1s. 6d. each.

Sufficient for 4 or 5 persons.

Seasonable from September to February.

CHICKEN OR FOWL PATTIES

Ingredients.—The remains of cold roast chicken or fowl; to every ¼ lb. of meat allow 2 oz. of ham, 3 tablespoonfuls of cream, 2 tablespoonfuls of veal gravy, ½ teaspoonful of minced lemon-peel; cayenne, salt, and pepper to taste; 1 tablespoonful of lemon-juice, 1 oz. of butter rolled in flour; puff paste.

Mode.—Mince very small the white meat from a cold roast fowl, after removing all the skin; weigh it, and to every ¼ lb. of meat allow the above proportion of minced ham. Put these into a stewpan with the remaining ingredients, stir over the fire for 10 minutes or ¼ hour, taking care that the mixture does not burn. Roll out some puff paste about ¼ inch in thickness; line the patty-pans with this, put upon each a small piece of bread, and cover with another layer of paste; brush over with the yolk of an egg, and bake in a brisk oven for about ¼ hour. When done, cut a round piece out of the top, and, with a small spoon, take out the bread (be particular in not breaking the outside border of the crust), and fill the patties with the mixture.

Time.—¼ hour to prepare the meat; not quite ¼ hour to bake the crust.

Seasonable at any time.

Hatching.—Sometimes the chick within the shell is unable to break away from its prison; for the white of the egg will occasionally harden in the air to the consistence of joiners' glue, when the poor chick is in a terrible fix. An able writer says, "Assistance in hatching must not be rendered prematurely, and thence unnecessarily, but only in the case of the chick being plainly unable to release itself; then, indeed, an addition may probably be made to the brood, as great numbers are always lost in this way. The chick makes a circular fracture at the big end of the egg, and a section of about one-third of the length of the shell being separated, delivers the prisoner, provided there is no obstruction from adhesion of the body to the membrane which lines the shell. Between the body of the chick and the membrane of the shell there exists a viscous fluid, the white of the egg thickened with the intense heat of incubation, until it becomes a positive glue. When this happens, the feathers stick fast to the shell, and the chicks remain confined, and must perish, if not released."

The method of assistance to be rendered to chicks which have a difficulty in releasing themselves from the shell, is to take the egg in the hand, and dipping the finger or a piece of linen rag in warm water, to apply it to the fastened parts until they are loosened by the gluey substance becoming dissolved and separated from the feathers. The chick, then, being returned to the nest, will extricate itself,—a mode generally to be observed, since, if violence were used, it would prove fatal. Nevertheless, breaking the shell may sometimes be necessary; and separating with the fingers, as gently as may be, the membrane from the feathers, which are still to be moistened as mentioned above, to facilitate the operation. The points of small scissors may be useful, and when there is much resistance, as also apparent pain to the bird, the process must be conducted in the gentlest manner, and the shell separated into a number of small pieces. The signs of a need of assistance are the egg being partly pecked and chipped, and the cluck discontinuing its efforts for five of six hours. Weakness from cold may disable the chicken from commencing the operation of pecking the shell, which must then be artificially performed with a circular fracture, such as is made by the bird itself.

FRICASSEED FOWL

(Cold Meat Cookery)

Ingredients.—The remains of cold roast fowl, 1 strip of lemon-peel, 1 blade of pounded mace, 1 bunch of savoury herbs, 1 onion, pepper and salt to taste, 1 pint of water, 1 teaspoonful of flour, ¼ pint of cream, the yolks of 2 eggs.

Mode.—Carve the fowls into nice joints; make gravy of the trimmings and legs, by stewing them with the lemon-peel, mace, herbs, onion, seasoning, and water, until reduced to ½ pint; then strain, and put in the fowl. Warm it through, and thicken with a teaspoonful of flour; stir the yolks of the eggs into the cream; add these to the sauce, let it get thoroughly hot, but do not allow it to boil, or it will curdle.

Time.—1 hour to make the gravy, ¼ hour to warm the fowl.

Average cost, exclusive of the cold chicken, 8d.

Seasonable at any time.

LARK PIE

(An Entrée)

Ingredients.—A few thin slices of beef, the same of bacon, 9 larks, flour; for stuffing, 1 teacupful of bread crumbs, ½ teaspoonful of minced lemon-peel, 1 teaspoonful of minced parsley, 1 egg, salt and pepper to taste, 1 teaspoonful of chopped shalot, ½ pint of weak stock or water, puff-paste.

Mode.—Make a stuffing of bread crumbs, minced lemon-peel, parsley, and the yolk of an egg, all of which should be well mixed together; roll the larks in flour, and stuff them. Line the bottom of a pie-dish with a few slices of beef and bacon; over these place the larks, and season with salt, pepper, minced parsley, and chopped shalot, in the above proportion. Pour in the stock or water, cover with crust, and bake for an hour in a moderate oven. During the time the pie is baking, shake it 2 or 3 times, to assist in thickening the gravy, and serve very hot.

Time.—1 hour.

Average cost.—1s. 6d. a dozen.

Sufficient for 5 or 6 persons.

Seasonable.—In full season in November.

CHAPTER EIGHT

RECIPES FOR COOKING GAME

ROAST BLACK-COCK

Ingredients.—Black-cock, butter, toast.

Mode.—Let these birds hang for a few days, or they will be tough and tasteless, if not well kept. Pluck and draw them, and wipe the insides and outsides with a damp cloth, as washing spoils the flavour. Cut off the heads, and truss them, the same as a roast fowl, cutting off the toes, and scalding and peeling the feet. Trussing them with the head on, as shown in the engraving, is still practised by many cooks, but the former method is now considered the best. Put them down to a brisk fire, well baste them with butter, and serve with a piece of toast under, and a good gravy and bread sauce. After trussing, some cooks cover the breast with vine-leaves and slices of bacon, and then roast them. They should be served in the same manner and with the same accompaniments as with the plainly-roasted birds.

Time.—45 to 50 minutes.

Average cost.—from 5s. to 6s. the brace; but seldom bought.

Sufficient.—2 or 3 for a dish.

Seasonable from the middle of August to the end of December.

ROAST BLACK-COCK.

135

The Black-Cock, Heath-Cock, Moor-Fowl, or Heath-Poult.—This bird sometimes weighs as much as four pounds, and the hen about two. It is at present confined to the more northern parts of Britain, culture and extending population having united in driving it into more desolate regions, except, perhaps, in a few of the more wild and less-frequented portions of England. It may still be found in the New Forest, in Hampshire, Dartmoor, and Sedgmoor, in Devonshire, and among the hills of Somersetshire, contiguous to the latter. It may also be found in Staffordshire, in North Wales, and again in the north of England; but nowhere so plentiful as in some parts of the Highlands of Scotland. The males are hardly distinguishable from the females until they are about half-grown, when the black feathers begin to appear, first about the sides and breast. Their food consists of the tops of birch and heath, except when the mountain berries are ripe, at which period they eagerly and even voraciously pick the bilberries and cranberries from the bushes. Large numbers of these birds are found in Norway, almost rivalling the turkey in point of size. Some of them have begun to be imported into London, where they are vended in the shops; but the flavour of their flesh is not equal to that of the Scotch bird.

ROAST WILD DUCK

Ingredients.—Wild duck, flour, butter.

Mode.—Carefully pluck and draw them; Cut off the heads close to the necks, leaving sufficient skin to turn over, and do not cut off the feet; some twist each leg at the knuckle, and rest the claws on each side of the breast; others truss them as shown in our Illustration. Roast the birds before a quick fire, and, when they are first put down, let them remain for 5 minutes without basting (this will keep the gravy in); afterwards baste plentifully with butter, and a few minutes before serving dredge them lightly with flour; baste well, and send them to table nicely frothed, and full of gravy. If overdone, the birds will lose their flavour. Serve with a good gravy in the dish; and send to table with them a cut lemon. To take off the fishy taste which wild fowl sometimes have, baste them for a few minutes with hot water to which have been added an onion and a little salt; then take away the pan, and baste with butter.

Time.—When liked underdressed, 20 to 25 minutes; well done, 25 to 35 minutes.

Average cost, 4s. to 5s. the couple.

Sufficient,—2 for a dish.

Seasonable from November to February.

ROAST WILD DUCK.

137

THE WILD DUCK.

The Wild Duck.—The male of the wild duck is called a mallard; and the young ones are called flappers. The time to try to find a brood of these is about the month of July, among the rushes of the deepest and most retired parts of some brook or stream, where, if the old bird is sprung, it may be taken as a certainty that its brood is not far off. When once found, flappers are easily killed, as they attain their full growth before their wings are fledged. Consequently, the sport is more like hunting water-rats than shooting birds. When the flappers take wing, they assume the name of wild ducks, and about the month of August repair to the corn-fields, where they remain until they are disturbed by the harvest-people. They then frequent the rivers pretty early in the evening, and give excellent sport to those who have patience to wait for them. In order to know a wild duck, it is necessary only to look at the claws, which should be black.

ROAST GROUSE

Ingredients.—Grouse, butter, a thick slice of toasted bread.

Mode.—Let the birds hang as long as possible; pluck and draw them; wipe, but do not wash them, inside and out, and truss them without the head, the same as for a roast fowl. Many persons still continue to truss them with the head under the wing, but the former is now considered the most approved method. Put them down to a sharp clear fire; keep them well basted the whole of the time they are cooking, and serve them on a buttered toast, soaked in the dripping-pan, with a little melted butter poured over them, or with bread-sauce and gravy.

Time.—½ hour; if liked very thoroughly done, 35 minutes.

Average cost.—2s. to 2s. 6d. the brace; but seldom bought.

Sufficient.—2 for a dish.

Seasonable from the 12th of August to the beginning of December.

ROAST GROUSE.

Grouse.—These birds are divided into wood grouse, black grouse, red grouse, and white grouse. The wood grouse is further distinguished as the cock of the wood, or capercalzie, and is as large as the turkey, being about two feet nine inches in length, and weighing from twelve to fifteen pounds. The female is considerably less than the male, and, in the colour of her feathers, differs widely from the other. This beautiful species is found principally in lofty, mountainous regions, and is very rare in Great Britain; but in the pine forests of Russia, Sweden, and other northern countries, it is very common. In these it has its habitat, feeding on the cones of the trees, and the fruits of various kinds of plants, especially the berry of the juniper. Black grouse is also distinguished as black-game, or the black-cock. It is not larger than the common hen, and weighs only about four pounds. The female is about one-third less than the male, and also differs considerably from him in point of colour. Like the former, they are found chiefly in high situations, and are common in Russia, Siberia, and other northern countries. They are also found in the northern parts of Great Britain, feeding in winter on the various berries and fruits belonging to mountainous countries, and, in summer, frequently descending to the lower lands, to feed upon corn. The red grouse, gorcock, or moor-cock, weighs about nineteen ounces, and the female somewhat less. In the wild heathy tracts of the northern counties of England it is plentiful, also in Wales and the Highlands of Scotland. Mr. Pennant considered it peculiar to Britain, those found in the mountainous parts of Spain, France, and Italy, being only varieties of the same bird. White grouse, white game, or ptarmigan, is nearly the same size as the red grouse, and is found in lofty situations, where it supports itself in the severest weather. It is to be met with in most of the northern countries of Europe, and appears even in Greenland. In the Hebrides, Orkneys, and the Highlands of Scotland, it is also found; and sometimes, though rarely, among the fells of Northumberland and Cumberland. In winter they fly in flocks, and are so little familiar with the sight of man, that they are easily shot, and even snared. They feed on the wild produce of the hills, which sometimes imparts to their flesh a bitter but not unpalatable taste. According to Buffon, it is dark-coloured, and somewhat flavoured like the hare.

RED GROUSE.

ROAST PARTRIDGE

Ingredients.—Partridge, butter.

Choosing and Trussing.—Choose young birds, with dark-coloured bills and yellowish legs, and let them hang a few days, or there will be no flavour to the flesh, nor will it be tender. The time they should be kept, entirely depends on the taste of those for whom they are intended, as what some persons would consider delicious, would be to others disgusting and offensive. They may be trussed with or without the head, the latter mode being now considered the most fashionable. Pluck, draw, and wipe the partridge carefully inside and out; cut off the head, leaving sufficient skin on the neck to skewer back; bring the legs close to the breast, between it and the side-bones, and pass a skewer through the pinions and the thick part of the thighs. When the head is left on, it should be brought round and fixed on to the point of the skewer.

ROAST PARTRIDGE.

Mode.—When the bird is firmly and plumply trussed, roast it before a nice bright fire; keep it well basted, and a few minutes before serving, flour and froth it well. Dish it, and serve with gravy and bread sauce, and send to table hot and quickly. A little of the gravy should be poured over the bird.

Time.—25 to 35 minutes.

Average cost.—is 1s. 6d. to 2s. a brace.

Sufficient.—2 for a dish.

Seasonable from the 1st of September to the beginning of February.

PARTRIDGES.

The Partridge.—This bird is to be found in nearly all the temperate countries of Europe, but is most abundant in the Ukraine, although it is unable to bear the extremes of climate, whether hot or cold. It was formerly very common in France, and is considered a table luxury in England. The instinct of this bird is frequently exemplified in a remarkable manner, for the preservation of its young. "I have seen it often," says a very celebrated writer, and an accurate observer of nature, "and once in particular, I saw an extraordinary instance of an old bird's solicitude to save its brood. As I was hunting with a young pointer, the dog ran on a brood of very small partridges; the old bird cried, fluttered, and ran tumbling along just before the dog's nose, till she had drawn him to a considerable distance, when she took wing, and flew still further off, but not out of the field; on this the dog returned to me, near the place where the young ones lay concealed in the grass, which the old bird no sooner perceived than she flew back to us, settled just before the dog's nose again, and by rolling and tumbling about, drew off his attention from her young, and thus preserved her brood a second time. I have also seen, when a kite has been hovering over a covey of young partridges, the old birds fly up at the bird of prey, screaming and fighting with all their might to preserve their brood." Partridges should be chosen young; if old, they are valueless. The young ones are generally known by their yellow legs and dark-coloured bills.

ROAST PHEASANT

Ingredients.—Pheasant, flour, butter.

Choosing and Trussing.—Old pheasants may be known by the length and sharpness of their spurs; in young ones they are short and blunt. The cock bird is generally reckoned the best, except when the hen is with egg. They should hang some time before they are dressed, as, if they are cooked fresh, the flesh will be exceedingly dry and tasteless. After the bird is plucked and drawn, wipe the inside with a damp cloth, and truss it in the same manner as partridge.

ROAST PHEASANT.

Mode.—Roast it before a brisk fire, keep it well basted, and flour and froth it nicely. Serve with brown gravy, a little of which should be poured round the bird, and a tureen of bread sauce. 2 or 3 of the pheasant's best tail-feathers are sometimes stuck in the tail as an ornament; but the fashion is not much to be commended.

Time.—½ to 1 hour, according to the size.

Average cost.—2s. 6d. to 3s. each.

Sufficient.—1 for a dish.

Seasonable from the 1st of October to the beginning of February.

The Pheasant.—This beautiful bird is said to have been discovered by the Argonauts on the banks of the Phasis, near Mount Ararat, in their expedition to Colchis. It is common, however, in almost all the southern parts of the European continent, and has been long naturalised in the warmest and most woody counties of England. It is very common in France; indeed, so common as to be esteemed a nuisance by the farmers. Although it has been domesticated, this is not easily accomplished, nor is its flesh so palatable then as it is in the wild state. Mr. Ude says—"It is not often that pheasants are met with possessing that exquisite taste which is acquired only by long keeping, as the damp of this climate prevents their being kept as long as they are in other countries. The hens, in general, are the most delicate. The cocks show their age by their spurs. They are only fit to be eaten when the blood begins to run from the bill, which is commonly six days or a week after they have been killed. The flesh is white, tender, and has a good flavour, if you keep it long enough; if not, it is not much different from that of a common fowl or hen."

THE PHEASANT.

146

STEWED VENISON

Ingredients.—A shoulder of venison, a few slices of mutton fat, 2 glasses of port wine, pepper and allspice to taste, 1½ pint of weak stock or gravy, ½ teaspoonful of whole pepper, ½ teaspoonful of whole allspice.

Mode.—Hang the venison till tender; take out the bone, flatten the meat with a rolling-pin, and place over it a few slices of mutton fat, which have been previously soaked for 2 or 3 hours in port wine; sprinkle these with a little fine allspice and pepper, roll the meat up, and bind and tie it securely. Put it into a stewpan with the bone and the above proportion of weak stock or gravy, whole allspice, black pepper, and port wine; cover the lid down closely, and simmer, very gently, from 3½ to 4 hours. When quite tender, take off the tape, and dish the meat; strain the gravy over it, and send it to table with red-currant jelly. Unless the joint is very fat, the above is the best mode of cooking it.

Time.—3½ to 4 hours.

Average cost.—1s. 4d. to 1s. 6d. per lb.

Sufficient for 10 or 12 persons.

Seasonable.—Buck venison, from June to Michaelmas; doe venison, from November to the end of January.

The Roebuck.—This is the *Certuscapreolus*, or common roe, and is of a reddish-brown colour. It is an inhabitant of Asia, as well as of Europe. It has great grace in its movements, and stands about two feet seven inches high, and has a length of about three feet nine. The extent of its horns is from six to eight inches.

THE ROEBUCK.

GAME ENTRÉES

HASHED GAME
(Cold Meat Cookery)
Ingredients.—The remains of cold game, 1 onion stuck with 3 cloves, a few whole peppers, a strip of lemon-peel, salt to taste, thickening of butter and flour, 1 glass of port wine, 1 tablespoonful of lemon-juice, 1 tablespoonful of ketchup, 1 pint of water or weak stock.
Mode.—Cut the remains of cold game into joints, reserve the best pieces, and the inferior ones and trimmings put into a stewpan with the onion, pepper, lemon-peel, salt, and water or weak stock; stew these for about an hour, and strain the gravy; thicken it with butter and flour; add the wine, lemon-juice, and ketchup; lay in the pieces of game, and let them gradually warm through by the side of the fire; do not allow it to boil, or the game will be hard. When on the point of simmering, serve, and garnish the dish with sippets of toasted bread.
Time.—Altogether 1¼ hour.
Seasonable from August to March.

Note.—Any kind of game may be hashed by the above recipe, and the flavour may be varied by adding flavoured vinegars, curry powder, &c.; but we cannot recommend these latter ingredients, as a dish of game should really have a gamy taste; and if too many sauces, essences, &c., are added to the gravy, they quite overpower and destroy the flavour the dish should possess.

JUGGED HARE

(*Very Good*)

Ingredients.—1 hare, 1½ lb. of gravy beef, ½ lb. of butter, 1 onion, 1 lemon, 6 cloves; pepper, cayenne, and salt to taste; ½ pint of port wine.

Mode.—Skin, paunch, and wash the hare, cut it into pieces, dredge them with flour, and fry in boiling butter. Have ready 1½ pint of gravy, made from the above proportion of beef, and thickened with a little flour. Put this into a jar; add the pieces of fried hare, an onion stuck with six cloves, a lemon peeled and cut in half, and a good seasoning of pepper, cayenne, and salt; cover the jar down tightly, put it up to the neck into a stewpan of boiling water, and let it stew until the hare is quite tender, taking care to keep the water boiling. When nearly done, pour in the wine, and add a few forcemeat balls: these must be fried or baked in the oven for a few minutes before they are put to the gravy. Serve with red-currant jelly.

Time.—3½ to 4 hours. If the hare is very old, allow 4½ hours.

Average cost.—7s.

Sufficient for 7 or 8 persons.

Seasonable from September to the end of February.

CHAPTER NINE

RECIPES FOR COOKING VEGETABLES

BOILED ARTICHOKES

Ingredients.—To each ½ gallon of water, allow 1 heaped tablespoonful of salt, a piece of soda the size of a shilling; artichokes.

Mode.—Wash the artichokes well in several waters; see that no insects remain about them, and trim away the leaves at the bottom. Cut off the stems and put them into *boiling* water, to which have been added salt and soda in the above proportion. Keep the saucepan uncovered, and let them boil quickly until tender; ascertain when they are done by thrusting a fork in them, or by trying if the leaves can be easily removed. Take them out, let them drain for a minute or 2, and serve in a napkin, or with a little white sauce poured over. A tureen of melted butter should accompany them. This vegetable, unlike any other, is considered better for being gathered 2 or 3 days; but they must be well soaked and washed previous to dressing.

Time.—20 to 25 minutes, after the water boils.

Sufficient.—a dish of 5 or 6 for 4 persons.

Seasonable from July to the beginning of September.

ARTICHOKES.

153

The Compositae, or Composite Flowers.—This family is so extensive, as to contain nearly a twelfth part of the whole of the vegetable kingdom. It embraces about 9,000 species, distributed over almost every country; and new discoveries are constantly being made and added to the number. Towards the poles their numbers diminish, and slightly, also, towards the equator; but they abound in the tropical and sub-tropical islands, and in the tracts of continent not far from the sea-shore. Among esculent vegetables, the Lettuce, Salsify, Scorzonera, Cardoon, and Artichoke belong to the family.

CARDOON ARTICHOKE.

BOILED JERUSALEM ARTICHOKES

Ingredients.—To each 1 gallon of water allow 1 heaped tablespoonful of salt; artichokes.

Mode.—Wash, peel, and shape the artichokes in a round or oval form, and put them into a saucepan with sufficient cold water to cover them, salted in the above proportion. Let them boil gently until tender; take them up, drain them, and serve them in a napkin, or plain, whichever mode is preferred; send to table with them a tureen of melted butter or cream sauce, a little of which may be poured over the artichokes when they are *not* served in a napkin.

Time.—About 20 minutes after the water boils.

Average cost.— 2d. per lb.

Sufficient.—10 for a dish for 6 persons.

Seasonable from September to June.

Uses of the Jerusalem Artichoke.—This being a tuberous-rooted plant, with leafy stems from four to six feet high, it is alleged that its tops will afford as much fodder per acre as a crop of oats, or more, and its roots half as many tubers as an ordinary crop of potatoes. The tubers, being abundant in the market-gardens, are to be had at little more than the price of potatoes. The fibres of the stems may be separated by maceration, and manufactured into cordage or cloth; and this is said to be done in some parts of the north and west of France, as about Hagenau, where this plant, on the poor sandy soils, is an object of field culture.

BOILED ASPARAGUS

Ingredients.—To each ½ gallon of water allow 1 heaped tablespoonful of salt; asparagus.

Mode.—Asparagus should be dressed as soon as possible after it is cut, although it may be kept for a day or 2 by putting the stalks into cold water; yet, to be good, like every other vegetable, it cannot be cooked too fresh. Scrape the white part of the stems, *beginning* from the *head*, and throw them into cold water; then tie them into bundles of about 20 each, keeping the heads all one way, and cut the stalks evenly, that they may all be the same length; put them into boiling water, with salt in the above proportion; keep them boiling quickly until tender, with the saucepan uncovered. When the asparagus is done, dish it upon toast, which should be dipped in the water it was cooked in, and leave the white ends outwards each way, with the points meeting in the middle. Serve with a tureen of melted butter.

Time.—15 to 18 minutes after the water boils.

Average cost, in full season, 2s. 6d. the 100 heads.

Sufficient.—Allow about 50 heads for 4 or 5 persons.

Seasonable.—May be had, forced, from January but cheapest in May, June, and July.

Asparagus.—This plant belongs to the variously-featured family of the order *Liliaceae*, which, in the temperate regions of both hemispheres, are most abundant, and, between the tropics, gigantic in size and arborescent in form. Asparagus is a native of Great Britain, and is found on various parts of the seacoast, and in the fens of Lincolnshire. At Kynarve Cove, in Cornwall, there is an island called "Asparagus Island," from the abundance in which it is there found. The uses to which the young shoots are applied, and the manure in which they are cultivated in order to bring them to the highest state of excellence, have been a study with many kitchen-gardeners.

BOILED BROAD OR WINDSOR BEANS

Ingredients.—To each ½ gallon of water, allow 1 heaped tablespoonful of salt; beans.

Mode.—This is a favourite vegetable with many persons, but to be nice, should be young and freshly gathered. After shelling the beans, put them into *boiling* water, salted in the above proportion, and let them boil rapidly until tender. Drain them well in a colander; dish, and serve with them separately a tureen of parsley and butter. Boiled bacon should always accompany this vegetable, but the beans should be cooked separately. It is usually served with the beans laid round, and the parsley and butter in a tureen. Beans also make an excellent garnish to a ham, and when used for this purpose, if very old, should have their skins removed.

Time.—Very young beans, 15 minutes; when of a moderate size, 20 to 25 minutes, or longer.

Average cost, unshelled, 6d. per peck.

Sufficient.—Allow one peck for 6 or 7 persons.

Seasonable in July and August.

BOILED BEETROOT

Ingredients.—Beetroot, boiling water.

Mode.—When large, young, and juicy, this vegetable makes a very excellent addition to winter salads, and may easily be converted into an economical and quickly-made pickle. Beetroot is more frequently served cold than hot: when the latter mode is preferred, melted butter should be sent to table with it. It may also be stewed with button onions, or boiled and served with roasted onions. Wash the beets thoroughly; but do not prick or break the skin before they are cooked, or they would lose their beautiful colour in boiling. Put them into boiling water, and let them boil until tender, keeping them well covered. If to be served hot, remove the peel quickly, cut the beetroot into thick slices, and send to table melted butter. For salads, pickle, &c., let the root cool, then peel, and cut it into slices.

Time.—Small beetroot, 1½ to 2 hours; large, 2½ to 3 hours.

Average cost, in full season, 2d. each.

Seasonable.—May be had at any time.

BEETROOT.

Beetroot.—The geographical distribution of the order Saltworts (*Salxolaceae*), to which beetroot belongs, is most common in extra-tropical and temperate regions, where they are common weeds, frequenting waste places, among rubbish, and on marshes by the seashore. In the tropics they are rare. They are characterized by the large quantities of mucilage, sugar, starch, and alkaline salts which are found in them. Many of them are used as potherbs, and some are emetic and vermifuge in their medicinal properties. The *root* of *garden* or red beet is exceedingly wholesome and nutritious, and Dr. Lyon Playfair has recommended that a good brown bread may be made by rasping down this root with an equal quantity of flour. He says that the average quality of flour contains about twelve per cent. of azotized principles adapted for the formation of flesh, and the average quality of beet contains about two per cent. of the same materials.

BOILED CABBAGE

Ingredients.—To each ½ gallon of water allow 1 heaped tablespoonful of salt; a *very small* piece of soda.

Mode.—Pick off all the dead outside leaves, cut off as much of the stalk as possible, and cut the cabbages across twice, at the stalk end; if they should be very large, quarter them. Wash them well in cold water, place them in a colander, and drain; then put them into *plenty* of *fast-boiling* water, to which have been added salt and soda in the above proportions. Stir them down once or twice in the water, keep the pan uncovered, and let them boil quickly until tender. The instant they are done, take them up into a colander, place a plate over them, let them thoroughly drain, dish, and serve.

Time.—Large cabbages, or savoys, ½ to ¾ hour, young summer cabbage, 10 to 12 minutes, after the water boils.

Average cost.—2d. each in full season.

Sufficient.—2 large ones for 4 or 5 persons.

Seasonable.—Cabbages and sprouts of various kinds at any time.

The Cabbage Tribe; Their Origin.—Of all the tribes of the *Cruciferae* this is by far the most important. Its scientific name is *Brassiceae*, and it contains a collection of plants which, both in themselves and their products, occupy a prominent position in agriculture, commerce, and domestic economy. On the cliffs of Dover, and in many places on the coasts of Dorsetshire, Cornwall, and Yorkshire, there grows a wild plant, with variously-indented, much-waved, and loose spreading leaves, of a sea-green colour, and large yellow flowers. In spring, the leaves of this plant are collected by the inhabitants, who, after boiling them in two waters, to remove the saltness, use them as a vegetable along with their meat. This is the *Brassica oleracea* of science, the Wild Cabbage, or Colewort, from which have originated all the varieties of Cabbage, Cauliflower, Greens, and Brocoli.

STEWED RED CABBAGE

Ingredients.—1 red cabbage, a small slice of ham, ½ oz. of fresh butter, 1 pint of weak stock or broth, 1 gill of vinegar, salt and pepper to taste, 1 tablespoonful of pounded sugar.

Mode.—Cut the cabbage into very thin slices, put it into a stewpan, with the ham cut in dice, the butter, ½ pint of stock, and the vinegar; cover the pan closely, and let it stew for 1 hour. When it is very tender, add the remainder of the stock, a seasoning of salt and pepper, and the pounded sugar; mix all well together, stir over the fire until nearly all the liquor is dried away, and serve. Fried sausages are usually sent to table with this dish: they should be laid round and on the cabbage, as a garnish.

Time.—Rather more than 1 hour.

Average cost.—4d. each.

Sufficient for 4 persons.

Seasonable from September to January.

The Wild Cabbage, or Colewort.—This plant, as it is found on the sea-cliffs of England, presents us with the origin of the cabbage tribe in its simplest and normal form. In this state it is the true Collet, or Colewort, although the name is now applied to any young cabbage which has a loose and open heart.

BOILED CAULIFLOWERS

Ingredients.—To each ½ gallon of water allow 1 heaped tablespoonful of salt.

CAULIFLOWER.

Mode.—Choose cauliflowers that are close and white; trim off the decayed outside leaves, and cut the stalk off flat at the bottom. Open the flower a little in places to remove the insects, which generally are found about the stalk, and let the cauliflowers lie in salt and water for an hour previous to dressing them, with their heads downwards: this will effectually draw out all the vermin. Then put them into fast-boiling water, with the addition of salt in the above proportion, and let them boil briskly over a good fire, keeping the saucepan uncovered. The water should be well skimmed; and, when the cauliflowers are tender, take them up with a slice; let them drain, and, if large enough, place them upright in the dish.

Serve with plain melted butter, a little of which may be poured over the flower.

Time.—Small cauliflower, 12 to 15 minutes; large one, 20 to 25 minutes, after the water boils.

Average cost, for large cauliflowers, 6d. each.

Sufficient.—Allow 1 large cauliflower for 3 persons.

Seasonable from the beginning of June to the end of September.

STEWED CUCUMBERS WITH ONIONS

Ingredients.—6 cucumbers, 3 moderate-sized onions, not quite 1 pint of white stock, cayenne and salt to taste, the yolks of 2 eggs, a very little grated nutmeg. *Mode.*—Pare and slice the cucumbers, take out the seeds, and cut the onions into thin slices; put these both into a stewpan, with the stock, and let them boil for ¼ hour or longer, should the cucumbers be very large. Beat up the yolks of 2 eggs; stir these into the sauce; add the cayenne, salt, and grated nutmeg; bring it to the point of boiling, and serve. Do not allow the sauce to boil, or it will curdle. This is a favourite dish with lamb or mutton chops, rump-steaks, &c.

Time.—Altogether, 20 minutes.

Average cost.—when cheapest, 4d. each.

Sufficient for 6 or 7 persons.

Seasonable in July, August, and September; but may be had, forced, from the beginning of March.

The Melon.—This is another species of the cucumber, and is highly esteemed for its rich and delicious fruit. It was introduced to this country from Jamaica, in 1570; since which period it has continued to be cultivated. It was formerly called the Musk Melon.

ENDIVE

This vegetable, so beautiful in appearance, makes an excellent addition to winter salad, when lettuces and other salad herbs are not obtainable. It is usually placed in the centre of the dish, and looks remarkably pretty with slices of beetroot, hard-boiled eggs, and curled celery placed round it, so that the colours contrast nicely. In preparing it, carefully wash and cleanse it free from insects, which are generally found near the heart; remove any decayed or dead leaves, and dry it thoroughly by shaking in a cloth. This vegetable may also be served hot, stewed in cream, brown gravy, or butter; but when dressed thus, the sauce it is stewed in should not be very highly seasoned, as that would destroy and overpower the flavour of the vegetable.

Average cost.—1d. per head.

Sufficient.—1 head for a salad for 4 persons.

Seasonable from November to March.

ENDIVE.

Endive.—This is the *C. endivium* of science, and is much used as a salad. It belongs to the family of the *Compositae*, with Chicory, common Goats-beard, and others of the same genus. Withering states, that before the stems of the common Goats-beard shoot up the roots, boiled like asparagus, have the same flavour, and are nearly as nutritious. We are also informed by Villars that the children in Dauphiné universally eat the stems and leaves of the young plant before the flowers appear, with great avidity. The fresh juice of these tender herbs is said to be the best solvent of bile.

HORSERADISH

This root, scraped, is always served with hot roast beef, and is used for garnishing many kinds of boiled fish. Let the horseradish remain in cold water for an hour; wash it well, and with a sharp knife scrape it into very thin shreds, commencing from the thick end of the root. Arrange some of it lightly in a small glass dish, and the remainder use for garnishing the joint: it should be placed in tufts round the border of the dish, with 1 or 2 bunches on the meat.

Average cost.—2d. per stick.

Seasonable from October to June.

HORSERADISH.

The Horseradish.—This belongs to the tribe *Alyssidae*, and is highly stimulant and exciting to the stomach. It has been recommended in chronic rheumatism, palsy, dropsical complaints, and in cases of enfeebled digestion. Its principal use, however, is as a condiment to promote appetite and excite the digestive organs. The horseradish contains sulphur to the extent of thirty per cent. in the

169

number of its elements; and it is to the presence of this quality that the metal vessels in which the radish is sometimes distilled, are turned into a black colour. It is one of the most powerful excitants and antiscorbutics we have, and forms the basis of several medical preparations, in the form of wines, tinctures, and syrups.

BROILED MUSHROOMS

(A Breakfast, Luncheon, or Supper Dish)

Ingredients.—Mushroom-flaps, pepper and salt to taste, butter, lemon-juice.

BROILED MUSHROOMS.

Mode.—Cleanse the mushrooms by wiping them with a piece of flannel and a little salt; cut off a portion of the stalk, and peel the tops: broil them over a clear fire, turning them once, and arrange them on a very hot dish. Put a small piece of butter on each mushroom, season with pepper and salt, and squeeze over them a few drops of lemon-juice. Place the dish before the fire, and when the butter is melted, serve very hot and quickly. Moderate-sized flaps are better suited to this mode of cooking than the buttons: the latter are better in stews.

Time.—10 minutes for medium-sized mushrooms.

Average cost.—1d. each for large mushrooms.

Sufficient.—Allow 3 or 4 mushrooms to each person.

Seasonable.—Meadow mushrooms in September and October; cultivated mushrooms may be had at any time.

MUSHROOMS.

Varieties of the Mushroom.—The common mushroom found in our pastures is the *Agaricus campestris* of science, and another edible British species is *A. Georgii,* but *A. primulus* is affirmed to be the most delicious mushroom. The morel is *Morchella esculenta*, and *Tuber cibarium* is the common truffle. There is in New Zealand a long fungus, which grows from the head of a caterpillar, and which forms a horn, as it were, and is called *Sphaeria Robertsii*.

BAKED SPANISH ONIONS

Ingredients.—4 or 5 Spanish onions, salt, and water.

Mode.—Put the onions, with their skins on, into a saucepan of boiling water slightly salted, and let them boil quickly for an hour. Then take them out, wipe them thoroughly, wrap each one in a piece of paper separately, and bake them in a moderate oven for 2 hours, or longer should the onions be very large. They may be served in their skins, and eaten with a piece of cold butter and a seasoning of pepper and salt; or they may be peeled, and a good brown gravy poured over them.

Time.—1 hour to boil, 2 hours to bake.

Average cost, medium-sized, 2d. each.

Sufficient for 5 or 6 persons.

Seasonable from September to January.

The Genus Allium.—The Onion, like the Leek, Garlic, and Shalot, belongs to the genus *Allium*, which is a numerous species of vegetable; and every one of them possesses, more or less, a volatile and acrid penetrating principle, pricking the thin transparent membrane of the eyelids; and all are very similar in their properties. In the whole of them the bulb is the most active part, and any one of them may supply the place of the other; for they are all irritant, excitant, and vesicant. With many, the onion is a very great favourite, and is considered an extremely nutritive vegetable. The Spanish kind is frequently taken for supper, it being simply boiled, and then seasoned with salt, pepper, and butter. Some dredge on a little flour, but many prefer it without this.

PEASE PUDDING

Ingredients.—1½ pint of split peas, 2 oz. of butter, 2 eggs, pepper and salt to taste.

Mode.—Put the peas to soak over-night, in rain-water, and float off any that are wormeaten or discoloured. Tie them loosely in a clean cloth, leaving a little room for them to swell, and put them on to boil in cold rain-water, allowing 2½ hours after the water has simmered up. When the peas are tender, take them up and drain; rub them through a colander with a wooden spoon; add the butter, eggs, pepper, and salt; beat all well together for a few minutes, until the ingredients are well incorporated; then tie them tightly in a floured cloth; boil the pudding for another hour, turn it on to the dish, and serve very hot. This pudding should always be sent to table with boiled leg of pork, and is an exceedingly nice accompaniment to boiled beef.

Time.—2½ hours to boil the peas, tied loosely in the cloth; 1 hour for the pudding.

Average cost.—6d.

Sufficient for 7 or 8 persons.

Seasonable from September to March.

WINTER SALAD

Ingredients.—Endive, mustard-and-cress, boiled beetroot, 3 or 4 hard-boiled eggs, celery.

Mode.—The above ingredients form the principal constituents of a winter salad, and may be converted into a very pretty dish, by nicely contrasting the various colours, and by tastefully garnishing it. Shred the celery into thin pieces, after having carefully washed and cut away all wormeaten pieces; cleanse the endive and mustard-and-cress free from grit, and arrange these high in the centre of a salad-bowl or dish; garnish with the hard-boiled eggs and beetroot, both of which should be cut in slices; and pour into the dish, but not over the salad, with salad dressing. Never dress a salad long before it is required for table, as, by standing, it loses its freshness and pretty crisp and light appearance; the sauce, however, may always be prepared a few hours beforehand, and when required for use, the herbs laid lightly over it.

Average cost.—9d. for a salad for 5 or 6 persons.

Sufficient for 5 or 6 persons.

Seasonable from the end of September to March.

Salads.—Salads are raw vegetables, of which, among us, the lettuce is the most generally used; several others, however, such as cresses, celery, onions, beetroot, &c., are occasionally employed. As vegetables eaten in a raw state are apt to ferment on the stomach, and as they have very little stimulative power upon that organ, they are usually dressed with some condiments, such as pepper, vinegar, salt, mustard, and oil. Respecting the use of these, medical men disagree, especially in reference to oil, which is condemned by some and recommended by others.

SPINACH DRESSED WITH CREAM, à la Française

Ingredients.—2 pailfuls of spinach, 2 tablespoonfuls of salt, 2 oz. of butter, 8 tablespoonfuls of cream, 1 small teaspoonful of pounded sugar, a very little grated nutmeg.

Mode.—Boil and drain the spinach; chop it finely, and put it into a stewpan with the butter; stir over a gentle fire, and, when the butter has dried away, add the remaining ingredients, and simmer for about 5 minutes. Previously to adding the cream, boil it first, in case it should curdle. Serve on a hot dish, and garnish either with sippets of toasted bread or leaves of puff-paste.

Time.—10 to 15 minutes to boil the spinach; 10 minutes to stew with the cream.

Average cost for the above quantity, 8d.

Sufficient for 5 or 6 persons.

Seasonable.—Spring spinach from March to July; winter spinach from November to March.

SPINACH.

Spinach.—This is a Persian plant. It has been cultivated in our gardens about two hundred years, and is the most wholesome of vegetables. It is not very nutritious, but is very easily digested. It is very light and laxative. Wonderful properties have been ascribed to spinach. It is an excellent vegetable, and very beneficial to health. Plainly dressed, it is a resource for the poor; prepared luxuriantly, it is a choice dish for the rich. Spinach belongs to a sub-order of the *Salsolaceae*, or saltworts, and is classified under the head of *Spirolobeae*, with leaves shaped like worms, and of a succulent kind. In its geographical distribution it is commonly found in extratropical and temperate regions, where they grow as weeds in waste places, and among rubbish, and in marshes by the seashore. In the tropics the order is rarely found. Many of them are used as potherbs, and some of them are emetic and vermifuge in their medicinal properties.

MASHED TURNIPS

Ingredients.—10 or 12 large turnips; to each ½ gallon of water allow 1 heaped tablespoonful of salt, 2 oz. of butter, cayenne or white pepper to taste.

Mode.—Pare the turnips, quarter them, and put them into boiling water, salted in the above proportion; boil them until tender; then drain them in a colander, and squeeze them as dry as possible by pressing them with the back of a large plate. When quite free from water, rub the turnips with a wooden spoon through the colander, and put them into a very clean saucepan; add the butter, white pepper, or cayenne, and, if necessary, a little salt. Keep stirring them over the fire until the butter is well mixed with them, and the turnips are thoroughly hot; dish, and serve. A little cream or milk added after the turnips are pressed through the colander, is an improvement to both the colour and flavour of this vegetable.

Time.—From ½ to ¾ hour to boil the turnips; 10 minutes to warm them through.

Average cost.—4d. per bunch.

Sufficient for 4 or 5 persons.

Seasonable.—May be had all the year; but in spring only good for flavouring gravies.

Vegetables Reduced to Purée.—Persons in the flower of youth, having healthy stomachs, and leading active lives, may eat all sorts of vegetables, without inconvenience, save, of course, in excess. The digestive functions possess great energy during the period of youth: the body, to develop itself, needs nourishment.

Physical exercise gives an appetite, which it is necessary to satisfy, and vegetables cannot resist the vigorous action of the gastric organs. As old proverb says, "At twenty one can digest iron." But for aged persons, the sedentary, or the delicate, it is quite otherwise. Then the gastric power has considerably diminished, the digestive organs have lost their energy, the process of digestion is consequently slower, and the least excess at table is followed by derangement of the stomach for several days. Those who generally digest vegetables with difficulty, should eat them reduced to a pulp or purée, that is to say, with their skins and tough fibres removed. Subjected to this process, vegetables which, when entire, would create flatulence and wind, are then comparatively harmless. Experience has established the rule, that nourishment is not complete without the alliance of meat with vegetables. We would also add, that the regime most favourable to health is found in variety: variety pleases the senses, monotony is disagreeable. The eye is fatigued by looking always on one object, the ear by listening to one sound, and the palate by tasting one flavour. It is the same with the stomach: consequently, variety of food is one of the essentials for securing good digestion.

FRIED VEGETABLE MARROW

Ingredients.—3 medium-sized vegetable marrows, egg and bread crumbs, hot lard.

Mode.—Peel, and boil the marrows until tender in salt and water; then drain them and cut them in quarters, and take out the seeds. When thoroughly drained, brush the marrows over with egg, and sprinkle with bread crumbs; have ready some hot lard, fry the marrow in this, and, when of a nice brown, dish; sprinkle over a little salt and pepper, and serve.

Time.—About ½ hour to boil the marrow, 7 minutes to fry it.

Average cost, in full season, 1s. per dozen.

Sufficient for 4 persons.

Seasonable in July, August, and September.

VEGETABLE-MARROW.

The Vegetable Marrow.—This vegetable is now extensively used, and belongs to the Cucurbits. It is the *C. ovifera* of science, and, like the melon, gourd, cucumber, and squash, is widely diffused in the tropical or warmer regions of the globe. Of the nature of this family we have already spoken when treating of the cucumber.

CHAPTER TEN

RECIPES FOR PUDDINGS, PASTRY, AND SWEET DISHES

VERY GOOD PUFF-PASTE

Ingredients.—To every lb. of flour allow 1 lb. of butter, and not quite ½ pint of water.

Mode.—Carefully weigh the flour and butter, and have the exact proportion; squeeze the butter well, to extract the water from it, and afterwards wring it in a clean cloth, that no moisture may remain. Sift the flour; see that it is perfectly dry, and proceed in the following manner to make the paste, using a very *clean* paste-board and rolling-pin:—Supposing the quantity to be 1 lb. of flour, work the whole into a smooth paste, with not quite ½ pint of water, using a knife to mix it with: the proportion of this latter ingredient must be regulated by the discretion of the cook; if too much be added, the paste, when baked, will be tough. Roll it out until it is of an equal thickness of about an inch; break 4 oz. of the butter into small pieces; place these on the paste, sift over it a little flour, fold it over, roll out again, and put another 4 oz. of butter. Repeat the rolling and buttering until the paste has been rolled out 4 times, or equal quantities of flour and butter have been used. Do not omit, every time the paste is rolled out, to dredge a little flour over that and the rolling-pin, to prevent both from sticking. Handle the paste as lightly as possible, and do not press heavily upon it with the rolling-pin. The next thing to be considered is the oven, as the baking of pastry requires particular attention. Do not put it into the oven until it is sufficiently hot to raise the paste; for the best-prepared paste, if not properly baked, will be good for nothing. Brushing the paste as often as rolled out, and the pieces of butter placed thereon, with the white of an egg, assists it to rise in *leaves* or *flakes*. As this is the great beauty of puff-paste, it is as well to try this method.

Average cost.—1s. 4d. per lb.

Butter.—About the second century of the Christian era, butter was placed by Galen amongst the useful medical agents; and about a century before him, Dioscorides mentioned that he had noticed that fresh butter, made of ewes' and goats' milk, was served at meals instead of oil, and that it took the place of fat in making pastry. Thus we have undoubted authority that, eighteen hundred years ago, there existed a knowledge of the useful qualities of butter. The Romans seem to have set about making it much as we do; for Pliny tells us, "Butter is made from milk; and the use of this element, so much sought after by barbarous nations, distinguished the rich from the common people. It is obtained principally from cows' milk; that from ewes is the fattest; goats also supply some. It is produced by agitating the milk in long vessels with narrow openings: a little water is added."

VERY GOOD SHORT CRUST for Fruit Tarts

Ingredients.—To every lb. of flour allow ¾ lb. of butter, 1 tablespoonful of sifted sugar, ⅛ pint of water.

Mode.—Rub the butter into the flour, after having ascertained that the latter is perfectly dry; add the sugar, and mix the whole into a stiff paste, with about one-third of a pint of water. Roll it out 2 or 3 times, folding the paste over each time, and it will be ready for use.

Average cost.—1s. 1d. per lb.

SUET CRUST, for Pies or Puddings

Ingredients.—To every lb. of flour allow 5 or 6 oz. of beef suet, ½ pint of water.

Mode.—Free the suet from skin and shreds; chop it extremely fine, and rub it well into the flour; work the whole to a smooth paste with the above proportion of water; roll it out, and it is ready for use. This crust is quite rich enough for ordinary purposes, but when a better one is desired, use from ½ to ¾ lb. of suet to every lb. of flour. Some cooks, for rich crusts, pound the suet in a mortar, with a small quantity of butter. It should then be laid on the paste in small pieces, the same as for puff-crust, and will be found exceedingly nice for hot tarts. 5 oz. of suet to every lb. of flour will make a very good crust; and even ¼ lb. will answer very well for children, or where the crust is wanted very plain.

Average cost.—5d. per lb.

SMALL ALMOND PUDDINGS

Ingredients.—½ lb. of sweet almonds, 6 bitter ones, ¼ lb. of butter, 4 eggs, 2 tablespoonfuls of sifted sugar, 2 tablespoonfuls of cream, 1 tablespoonful of brandy.

ALMOND PUDDINGS.

Mode.—Blanch and pound the almonds to a smooth paste with a spoonful of water; warm the butter, mix the almonds with this, and add the other ingredients, leaving out the whites of 2 eggs, and be particular that these are well beaten. Mix well, butter some cups, half fill them, and bake the puddings from 20 minutes to ½ hour. Turn them out on a dish, and serve with sweet sauce.

Time.—20 minutes to ½ hour.

Average cost.—1s.

Sufficient for 4 or 5 persons.

Seasonable at any time.

AUNT NELLY'S PUDDING

Ingredients.—½ lb. of flour, ½ lb. of treacle, ½ lb. of suet, the rind and juice of 1 lemon, a few strips of candied lemon-peel, 3 tablespoonfuls of cream, 2 eggs.

Mode.—Chop the suet finely; mix with it the flour, treacle, lemon-peel minced, and candied lemon-peel; add the cream, lemon-juice, and 2 well-beaten eggs; beat the pudding well, put it into a buttered basin, tie it down with a cloth, and boil from 3½ to 4 hours.

Time.—3½ to 4 hours.

Average cost.—1s. 2d.

Sufficient for 5 or 6 persons.

Seasonable at any time, but more suitable for a winter pudding.

Treacle or Molasses.—Treacle is the uncrystallizable part of the saccharine juice drained from the Muscovado sugar, and is either naturally so or rendered uncrystallizable through some defect in the process of boiling. As it contains a large quantity of sweet or saccharine principle and is cheap, it is of great use as an article of domestic economy. Children are especially fond of it; and it is accounted wholesome. It is also useful for making beer, rum, and the very dark syrups.

APPLE CHEESECAKES

Ingredients.—½ lb. of apple pulp, ¼ lb. of sifted sugar, ¼ lb. of butter, 4 eggs, the rind and juice of 1 lemon.
Mode.—Pare, core, and boil sufficient apples to make ½ lb. when cooked; add to these the sugar, the butter, which should be melted; the eggs, leaving out 2 of the whites, and take grated rind and juice of 1 lemon; stir the mixture well; line some patty-pans with puff-paste, put in the mixture, and bake about 20 minutes.
Time.—About 20 minutes.
Average cost, for the above quantity, with the paste, 1s. 2d.
Sufficient for about 18 or 20 cheesecakes.
Seasonable from August to March.

The Apple.—The most useful of all the British fruits is the apple, which is a native of Britain, and may be found in woods and hedges, in the form of the common wild crab, of which all our best apples are merely seminal varieties, produced by culture or particular circumstances. In most temperate climates it is very extensively cultivated, and in England, both as regards variety and quantity, it is excellent and abundant. Immense supplies are also imported from the United States and from France. The apples grown in the vicinity of New York are universally admitted to be the finest of any; but unless selected and packed with great care, they are apt to spoil before reaching England.

ALMA PUDDING

Ingredients.—½ lb. of fresh butter, ½ lb. of powdered sugar, ½ lb. of flour, ¼ lb. of currants, 4 eggs.

Mode.—Beat the butter to a thick cream, strew in, by degrees, the sugar, and mix both these well together; then dredge the flour in gradually, add the currants, and moisten with the eggs, which should be well beaten. When all the ingredients are well stirred and mixed, butter a mould that will hold the mixture exactly, tie it down with a cloth, put the pudding into boiling water, and boil for 5 hours; when turned out, strew some powdered sugar over it, and serve.

Time.—6 hours.

Average cost.—1s. 6d.

Sufficient for 5 or 6 persons.

Seasonable at any time.

A BACHELOR'S PUDDING

Ingredients.—4 oz. of grated bread, 4 oz. of currants, 4 oz. of apples, 2 oz. of sugar, 3 eggs, a few drops of essence of lemon, a little grated nutmeg.

Mode.—Pare, core, and mince the apples very finely, sufficient, when minced, to make 4 oz.; add to these the currants, which should be well washed, the grated bread, and sugar; whisk the eggs, beat these up with the remaining ingredients, and, when all is thoroughly mixed, put the pudding into a buttered basin, tie it down with a cloth, and boil for 3 hours.

Time.—3 hours.

Average cost.—9d.

Sufficient for 4 or 5 persons.

Seasonable from August to March.

BAKED BREAD PUDDING

Ingredients.—½ lb. of grated bread, 1 pint of milk, 4 eggs, 4 oz. of butter, 4 oz. of moist sugar, 2 oz. of candied peel, 6 bitter almonds, 1 tablespoonful of brandy.

Mode.—Put the milk into a stewpan, with the bitter almonds; let it infuse for ¼ hour; bring it to the boiling point; strain it on to the bread crumbs, and let these remain till cold; then add the eggs, which should be well whisked, the butter, sugar, and brandy, and beat the pudding well until all the ingredients are thoroughly mixed; line the bottom of a pie-dish with the candied peel sliced thin, put in the mixture, and bake for nearly ¾ hour.

Time.—Nearly ¾ hour.

Average cost.—1s. 4d.

Sufficient for 5 or 6 persons.

Seasonable at any time.

Note.—A few currants may be substituted for the candied peel, and will be found an excellent addition to this pudding: they should be beaten in with the mixture, and not laid at the bottom of the pie-dish.

BAKED CUSTARD PUDDING

Ingredients.—1½ pint of milk, the rind of ¼ lemon, ¼ lb. of moist sugar, 4 eggs.

Mode.—Put the milk into a saucepan with the sugar and lemon-rind, and let this infuse for about 4 hours, or until the milk is well flavoured; whisk the eggs, yolks and whites; pour the milk to them, stirring all the while; then have ready a pie-dish, lined at the edge with paste ready baked; strain the custard into the dish, grate a little nutmeg over the top, and bake in a *very slow* oven for about ½ hour, or rather longer. The flavour of this pudding may be varied by substituting bitter almonds for the lemon-rind; and it may be very much enriched by using half cream and half milk, and doubling the quantity of eggs.

Time.—½ to ¾ hour.

Average cost.—9d.

Sufficient for 5 or 6 persons.

Seasonable at any time.

Note.—This pudding is usually served cold with fruit tarts.

ICED PUDDING

(*Parisian Recipe*)

Ingredients.—½ lb. of sweet almonds, 2 oz. of bitter ones, ¾ lb. of sugar, 8 eggs, 1½ pint of milk.

Mode.—Blanch and dry the almonds thoroughly in a cloth, then pound them in a mortar until reduced to a smooth paste; add to these the well-beaten eggs, the sugar, and milk; stir these ingredients over the fire until they thicken, but do not allow them to boil; then strain and put the mixture into the freezing-pot; surround it with ice, and freeze it. When quite frozen, fill an iced-pudding mould, put on the lid, and keep the pudding in ice until required for table; then turn it out on the dish, and garnish it with a *compôte* of any fruit that may be preferred, pouring a little over the top of the pudding. This pudding may be flavoured with vanilla, Curaçoa, or Maraschino.

Time.—½ hour to freeze the mixture.

Seasonable.—Served all the year round.

ICED-PUDDING MOULD.

BAKED PLUM-PUDDING

Ingredients.—2 lbs. of flour, 1 lb. of currants, 1 lb. of raisins, 1 lb. of suet, 2 eggs, 1 pint of milk, a few slices of candied peel.

Mode.—Chop the suet finely; mix with it the flour, currants, stoned raisins, and candied peel; moisten with the well-beaten eggs, and add sufficient milk to make the pudding of the consistency of very thick batter. Put it into a buttered dish, and bake in a good oven from 2¼ to 2½ hours; turn it out, strew sifted sugar over, and serve. For a very plain pudding, use only half the quantity of fruit, omit the eggs, and substitute milk or water for them. The above ingredients make a large family pudding; for a small one, half the quantity would be found ample; but it must be baked quite 1½ hour.

Time.—Large pudding, 2¼ to 2½ hours; half the size, 1½ hour.

Average cost.—2s. 6d.

Sufficient for 9 or 10 persons.

Seasonable in winter.

Raisin Grape.—All the kinds of raisins have much the same virtues; they are nutritive and balsamic, but they are very subject to fermentation with juices of any kind; and hence, when eaten immoderately, they often bring on colics. There are many varieties of grape used for raisins; the fruit of Valencia is that mostly dried for culinary purposes, whilst most of the table kinds are grown in Malaga, and called Muscatels. The finest of all table raisins come from Provence or Italy; the most esteemed of all are those of Roquevaire; they are very large and very sweet. This sort is rarely eaten by any but the most wealthy. The dried Malaga, or Muscatel raisins, which come to this country packed in small boxes, and nicely preserved in bunches, are variable in their quality, but mostly of a rich flavour, when new, juicy, and of a deep purple hue.

CHRISTMAS PLUM-PUDDING

(*Very Good*)

Ingredients.—1½ lb. of raisins, ½ lb. of currants, ½ lb. of mixed peel, ¾ lb. of bread crumbs, ¾ lb. of suet, 8 eggs, 1 wineglassful of brandy.

CHRISTMAS PLUM-PUDDING IN MOULD.

Mode.—Stone and cut the raisins in halves, but do not chop them; wash, pick, and dry the currants, and mince the suet finely; cut the candied peel into thin slices, and grate down the bread into fine crumbs. When all these dry ingredients are prepared, mix them well together; then moisten the mixture with the eggs, which should be well beaten, and the brandy; stir well, that everything may be very thoroughly blended, and *press* the pudding into a buttered mould; tie it down tightly with a floured cloth, and boil for 5 or 6 hours. It may be boiled in a cloth without a mould, and will require the same time allowed for cooking. As Christmas puddings are usually made a few days before they are required for table, when the pudding is taken out of the pot, hang it up immediately, and put a plate or saucer underneath to catch the water that may drain from it. The day it is to be eaten, plunge it into boiling water, and keep it boiling for at least 2 hours; then turn it out of the mould, and serve with brandy-sauce. On Christmas-day a sprig of holly is usually placed in the middle of the pudding, and about a wineglassful of brandy poured round it, which, at the moment of serving, is lighted, and the pudding thus brought to table encircled in flame.

Time.—5 or 6 hours the first time of boiling; 2 hours the day it is to be served.

Average cost.— 4s.

Sufficient for a quart mould for 7 or 8 persons.

Seasonable on the 25th of December, and on various festive occasions till March.

Note.—Five or six of these puddings should be made at one time, as they will keep good for many weeks, and in cases where unexpected guests arrive, will be found an acceptable, and, as it only requires warming through, a quickly-prepared dish. Moulds of every shape and size are manufactured for these puddings, and may be purchased of Messrs. R. & J. Slack, 336, Strand.

YORKSHIRE PUDDING, to serve with hot Roast Beef

Ingredients.—1½ pint of milk, 6 *large* tablespoonfuls of flour, 3 eggs, 1 saltspoonful of salt.

Mode.—Put the flour into a basin with the salt, and stir gradually to this enough milk to make it into a stiff batter. When this is perfectly smooth, and all the lumps are well rubbed down, add the remainder of the milk and the eggs, which should be well beaten. Beat the mixture for a few minutes, and pour it into a shallow tin, which has been previously well rubbed with beef dripping. Put the pudding into the oven, and bake it for an hour; then, for another ½ hour, place it under the meat, to catch a little of the gravy that flows from it. Cut the pudding into small square pieces, put them on a hot dish, and serve. If the meat is baked, the pudding may at once be placed under it, resting the former on a small three-cornered stand.

Time.—1½ hour.
Average cost.—7d.
Sufficient for 5 or 6 persons.
Seasonable at any time.

YORKSHIRE PUDDING.

OPEN TART OF STRAWBERRY OR ANY OTHER KIND OF PRESERVE

Ingredients.—Trimmings of puff-paste, any kind of jam.

OPEN TART.

OPEN TART MOULD.

Mode.—Butter a tart-pan of the shape shown in the engraving, roll out the paste to the thickness of ½ inch, and line the pan with it; prick a few holes at the bottom with a fork, and bake the tart in a brisk oven from 10 to 15 minutes. Let the paste cool a little; then fill it with preserve, place a few stars or leaves on it, which have been previously cut out of the paste and baked, and the tart is ready for table. By making it in this manner, both the flavour and colour of the jam are preserved, which would otherwise be lost, were it baked in the oven on the paste; and, besides, so much jam is not required.

Time.—10 to 15 minutes.

Average cost.—8d.

Sufficient.—1 tart for 3 persons.

Seasonable at any time.

Strawberry.—The name of this favourite fruit is said to be derived from an ancient custom of putting straw beneath the fruit when it began to ripen, which is very useful to keep it moist and clean. The strawberry belongs to temperate and rather cold climates; and no fruit of these latitudes, that ripens without the aid of artificial heat, is at all comparable with it in point of flavour. The strawberry is widely diffused, being found in most parts of the world, particularly in Europe and America.

CHAPTER ELEVEN

RECIPES FOR CREAMS, JELLIES, &c.

THICK APPLE JELLY OR MARMALADE, for Entremets or Dessert Dishes

Ingredients.—Apples; to every lb. of pulp allow ¾ lb. of sugar; ½ teaspoonful of minced lemon-peel.

APPLE JELLY STUCK WITH ALMONDS.

Mode.—Peel, core, and boil the apples with only sufficient water to prevent them from burning; beat them to a pulp, and to every lb. of pulp allow the above proportion of sugar in lumps. Dip the lumps into water; put these into a saucepan, and boil till the syrup is thick and can be well skimmed; then add this syrup to the apple pulp, with the minced lemon-peel, and stir it over a quick fire for about 20 minutes, or until the apples cease to stick to the bottom of the pan. The jelly is then done, and may be poured into moulds which have been previously dipped in water, when it will turn out nicely for dessert or a side-dish; for the latter a little custard should be poured round, and it should be garnished with strips of citron or stuck with blanched almonds.
Time.—From ½ to ¾ hour to reduce the apples to a pulp; 20 minutes to boil after the sugar is added.

Sufficient.—1½ lb. of apples sufficient for a small mould.

Seasonable from July to March; but is best in September, October or November.

BLANC-MANGE

(*A Supper Dish*)

Ingredients.—1 pint of new milk, 1¼ oz. of isinglass, the rind of ½ lemon, ¼ lb. of loaf sugar, 10 bitter almonds, ½ oz. of sweet almonds, 1 pint of cream.

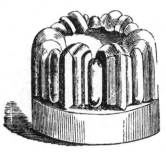

BLANC-MANGE MOULD.

Mode.—Put the milk into a saucepan, with the isinglass, lemon-rind, and sugar, and let these ingredients stand by the side of the fire until the milk is well flavoured; add the almonds, which should be blanched and pounded in a mortar to a paste, and let the milk just boil up; strain it through a fine sieve or muslin into a jug, add the cream, and stir the mixture occasionally until nearly cold. Let it stand for a few minutes, then pour it into the mould, which should be previously oiled with the purest salad-oil, or dipped in cold water. There will be a sediment at the bottom of the jug, which must not be poured into the mould, as, when turned out, it would very much disfigure the appearance of the blanc-mange. This blanc-mange may be made very much richer by using 1½ pint of cream, and melting the isinglass in ½ pint of boiling water. The flavour may also be very much varied by adding bay-leaves, laurel-leaves, or essence of vanilla, instead of the lemon-rind and almonds. Noyeau, Maraschino, Curaçoa, or any favourite liqueur, added in small proportions, very much enhances the flavour of this always favourite dish. In turning it out, just loosen the edges of the blanc-mange from the mould, place a dish on it, and turn it quickly over; it should come out easily, and the blanc-mange have a smooth glossy appearance when the mould is oiled, which it frequently has not when it is only dipped in water. It may be garnished as fancy dictates.

Time.—About 1½ hour to steep the lemon-rind and almonds in the milk.

Average cost, with cream at 1s. per pint, 3s. 3d.

Sufficient to fill a quart mould.

Seasonable at any time.

BOILED CUSTARDS

Ingredients.—1 pint of milk, 5 eggs, 3 oz. of loaf sugar, 3 laurel-leaves, or the rind of 4 lemons, or a few drops of essence of vanilla, 1 tablespoonful of brandy.

CUSTARDS IN GLASSES.

Mode.—Put the milk into a lined saucepan, with the sugar, and whichever of the above flavourings may be preferred (the lemon-rind flavours custards most deliciously), and let the milk steep by the side of the fire until it is well flavoured. Bring it to the point of boiling, then strain it into a basin; whisk the eggs well, and, when the milk has cooled a little, stir in the eggs, and *strain* this mixture into a jug. Place this jug in a saucepan of boiling water over the fire; keep stirring the custard *one way* until it thickens; but on no account allow it to reach the boiling-point, as it will instantly curdle and be full of lumps. Take it off the fire, stir in the brandy, and, when this is well mixed with the custard, pour it into glasses, which should be rather more than three-parts full; grate a little nutmeg over the top, and the dish is ready for table. To make custards look and eat better, ducks' eggs should be used, when obtainable; they add very much to the flavour and richness, and so many are not required as of the ordinary eggs, 4 ducks' eggs to the pint of milk making a delicious custard. When desired extremely rich and good, cream should be substituted for the milk, and double the quantity of eggs used, to those mentioned, omitting the whites.

Time.—½ hour to infuse the lemon-rind, about 10 minutes to stir the custard.

Average cost.—8d.

Sufficient to fill 8 custard-glasses.

Seasonable at any time.

CHOCOLATE CREAM

Ingredients.—3 oz. of grated chocolate, ¼ lb. of sugar, 1½ pint of cream, ½ oz. of clarified isinglass, the yolks of 6 eggs.

CREAM-MOULD.

Mode.—Beat the yolks of the eggs well; put them into a basin with the grated chocolate, the sugar, and 1 pint of the cream; stir these ingredients well together, pour them into a jug, and set this jug in a saucepan of boiling water; stir it one way until the mixture thickens, but *do not allow it to boil*, or it will curdle. Strain the cream through a sieve into a basin; stir in the isinglass and the other ½ pint of cream, which should be well whipped; mix all well together, and pour it into a mould which has been previously oiled with the purest salad-oil, and, if at hand, set it in ice until wanted for table.

Time.—About 10 minutes to stir the mixture over the fire.

Average cost.—4s. 6d, with cream at 1s. per pint.

Sufficient to fill a quart mould.

Seasonable at any time.

LEMON CREAM

Ingredients.—1 pint of cream, the yolks of 2 eggs, ¼ lb. of white sugar, 1 large lemon, 1 oz. of isinglass.

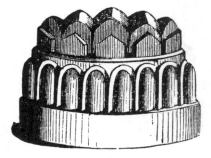

LEMON-CREAM MOULD.

Mode.—Put the cream into a *lined* saucepan with the sugar, lemon-peel, and isinglass, and simmer these over a gentle fire for about 10 minutes, stirring them all the time. Strain the cream into a jug, add the yolks of eggs, which should be well beaten, and put the jug into a saucepan of boiling water; stir the mixture one way until it thickens, *but do not allow it to boil*; take it off the fire, and keep stirring it until nearly cold. Strain the lemon-juice into a basin, gradually pour on it the cream, and *stir it well* until the juice is well mixed with it. Have ready a well-oiled mould, pour the cream into it, and let it remain until perfectly set. When required for table, loosen the edges with a small blunt knife, put a dish on the top of the mould, turn it over quickly, and the cream should easily slip away.

214

Time.—10 minutes to boil the cream; about 10 minutes to stir it over the fire in the jug.

Average cost, with cream at 1s. per pint, and the best isinglass, 2s. 6d.

Sufficient to fill 1½-pint mould.

Seasonable at any time.

LIQUEUR JELLY

Ingredients.—1 lb. of lump sugar, 2 oz. of isinglass, 1½ pint of water, the juice of 2 lemons, ¼ pint of liqueur.

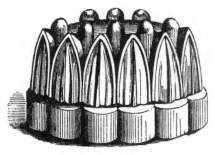

OVAL JELLY-MOULD.

Mode.—Put the sugar, with 1 pint of the water, into a stewpan, and boil them gently by the side of the fire until there is no scum remaining, which must be carefully removed as fast as it rises. Boil the isinglass with the other ½ pint of water, and skim it carefully in the same manner. Strain the lemon-juice, and add it, with the clarified isinglass, to the syrup; put in the liqueur, and bring the whole to the boiling-point. Let the saucepan remain covered by the side of the fire for a few minutes; then pour the jelly through a bag, put it into a mould, and set the mould in ice until required for table. Dip the mould in hot water, wipe the outside, loosen the jelly by passing a knife round the edges, and turn it out carefully on a dish. Noyeau, Maraschino, Curaçoa, brandy, or any kind of liqueur, answers for this jelly; and, when made with isinglass, liqueur jellies are usually prepared as directed above.

Time.—10 minutes to boil the sugar and water.

Average cost, with the best isinglass, 3s. 6d.

Sufficient to fill a quart mould.

Seasonable at any time.

MERINGUES

Ingredients.—½ lb. of pounded sugar, the whites of 4 eggs.

MERINGUES.

Mode.—Whisk the whites of the eggs to a stiff froth, and, with a wooden spoon, stir in *quickly* the pounded sugar; and have some boards thick enough to put in the oven to prevent the bottom of the meringues from acquiring too much colour. Cut some strips of paper about 2 inches wide; place this paper on the board, and drop a tablespoonful at a time of the mixture on the paper, taking care to let all the meringues be the same size. In dropping it from the spoon, give the mixture the form of an egg, and keep the meringues about 2 inches apart from each other on the paper. Strew over them some sifted sugar, and bake in a moderate oven for ½ hour. As soon as they begin to colour, remove them from the oven; take each slip of paper by the two ends, and turn it gently on the table, and, with a small spoon, take out the soft part of each meringue. Spread some clean paper on the board, turn the meringues upside down, and put them into the oven to harden and brown on the other side. When required for table, fill them with whipped cream, flavoured with liqueur or vanilla, and sweetened with pounded sugar. Join two of the meringues together, and pile them high in the dish, as shown in the annexed drawing. To vary their appearance, finely-chopped almonds or currants may be strewn over them before the sugar is sprinkled over; and they may be garnished with any bright-coloured preserve. Great expedition is necessary in making this sweet dish; as, if the meringues are not put into the oven as soon as the sugar and eggs are mixed, the former melts, and the mixture would run on the paper, instead of keeping its egg-shape. The sweeter the meringues are made, the crisper will they be; but, if there is not sufficient sugar mixed with them, they will most likely be tough. They are sometimes coloured with cochineal; and, if kept well covered in a dry place, will remain good for a month or 6 weeks.

Time.—Altogether, about ½ hour.

Average cost, with the cream and flavouring, 1s.

Sufficient to make 2 dozen meringues.

Seasonable at any time.

OPEN JELLY WITH WHIPPED CREAM

(*A Very Pretty Dish*)

Ingredients.—1½ pint of jelly, ½ pint of cream, 1 glass of sherry, sugar to taste.

OPEN JELLY WITH WHIPPED CREAM.

Mode.—Make the above proportion of calf's-feet or isinglass jelly, colouring and flavouring it in any way that may be preferred; soak a mould, open in the centre, for about ½ hour in cold water; fill it with the jelly, and let it remain in a cool place until perfectly set; then turn it out on a dish; fill the centre with whipped cream, flavoured with sherry and sweetened with pounded sugar; pile this cream high in the centre, and serve. The jelly should be made of rather a dark colour, to contrast nicely with the cream.

Time.—¾ hour.

Average cost.—3s. 6d.

Sufficient to fill 1½-pint mould.

Seasonable at any time.

RASPBERRY CREAM

Ingredients.—¾ pint of milk, ¾ pint of cream, 1½ oz. of isinglass, raspberry jelly, sugar to taste, 2 tablespoonfuls of brandy.

RASPBERRY-CREAM MOULD.

Mode.—Boil the milk, cream, and isinglass together for ¼ hour, or until the latter is melted, and strain it through a hair sieve into a basin. Let it cool a little; then add to it sufficient raspberry jelly, which, when melted, would make ¼ pint, and stir well till the ingredients are thoroughly mixed. If not sufficiently sweet, add a little pounded sugar with the brandy; whisk the mixture well until nearly cold, put it into a well-oiled mould, and set it in a cool place till perfectly set. Raspberry jam may be substituted for the jelly, but must be melted, and rubbed through a sieve, to free it from seeds: in summer, the juice of the fresh fruit may be used, by slightly mashing it with a wooden spoon, and sprinkling sugar over it; the juice that flows from the fruit should then be used for mixing with the cream. If the colour should not be very good, a few drops of prepared cochineal may be added to improve its appearance.

Time.—¼ hour to boil the cream and isinglass.

Average cost, with cream at 1s. per pint, and the best isinglass, 3s.

Sufficient to fill a quart mould.

Seasonable, with jelly, at any time.

Note.—Strawberry cream may be made in precisely the same manner, substituting strawberry jam or jelly for the raspberry.

TIPSY CAKE

Ingredients.—1 moulded sponge- or Savoy-cake, sufficient sweet wine or sherry to soak it, 6 tablespoonfuls of brandy, 2 oz. of sweet almonds, 1 pint of rich custard.

TIPSY CAKE.

Mode.—Procure a cake that is 3 or 4 days old,—either sponge, Savoy, or rice answering for the purpose of a tipsy cake. Cut the bottom of the cake level, to make it stand firm in the dish; make a small hole in the centre, and pour in and over the cake sufficient sweet wine or sherry, mixed with the above proportion of brandy, to soak it nicely. When the cake is well soaked, blanch and cut the almonds into strips, stick them all over the cake, and pour round it a good custard, allowing 8 eggs instead of 5 to the pint of milk. The cakes are sometimes crumbled and soaked, and a whipped cream heaped over them, the same as for trifles.

Time.—About 2 hours to soak the cake.

Average cost.—4s. 6d.

Sufficient for 1 dish.

Seasonable at any time.

Almond.—The almond-tree is a native of warmer climates than Britain, and is indigenous to the northern parts of Africa and Asia; but it is now commonly cultivated in Italy, Spain, and the south of France. It is not usually grown in Britain, and the fruit seldom ripens in this country: it is much admired for the beauty of its blossoms. In the form of its leaves and blossoms it strongly resembles the peach-tree, and is included in the same genus by botanists; but the fruit, instead of presenting a delicious pulp like the peach, shrivels up as it ripens, and becomes only a tough coriaceous covering to the stone inclosing the eatable kernel, which is surrounded by a thin bitter skin. It flowers early in the spring, and produces fruit in August. There are two sorts of almonds,—sweet and bitter; but they are considered to be only varieties of the species; and though the qualities of the kernels are very different, they are not distinguishable by their appearance.

CHAPTER TWELVE

RECIPES FOR PRESERVES AND STORE SAUCES

CHERRY JAM

Ingredients.—To every lb. of fruit, weighed before stoning, allow ½ lb. of sugar; to every 6 lbs. of fruit allow 1 pint of red-currant juice, and to every pint of juice 1 lb. of sugar.

Mode.—Weigh the fruit before stoning, and allow half the weight of sugar; stone the cherries, and boil them in a preserving-pan until nearly all the juice is dried up; then add the sugar, which should be crushed to powder, and the currant-juice, allowing 1 pint to every 6 lbs. of cherries (original weight), and 1 lb. of sugar to every pint of juice. Boil all together until it jellies, which will be in from 20 minutes to ½ hour; skim the jam well, keep it well stirred, and, a few minutes before it is done, crack some of the stones, and add the kernels: these impart a very delicious flavour to the jam.

Time.—According to the quality of the cherries, from ¾ to 1 hour to boil them; 20 minutes to ½ hour with the sugar.

Average cost.—from 7d. to 8d. per lb. pot.

Sufficient.—1 pint of fruit for a lb. pot of jam.

Seasonable.—Make this in July or August.

RED-CURRANT JAM

Ingredients.—To every lb. of fruit allow ¾ lb. of loaf sugar.

Mode.—Let the fruit be gathered on a fine day; weigh it, and then strip the currants from the stalks; put them into a preserving-pan with sugar in the above proportion; stir them, and boil them for about ¾ hour. Carefully remove the scum as it rises. Put the jam into pots, and, when cold, cover with oiled papers; over these put a piece of tissue-paper brushed over on both sides with the white of an egg; press the paper round the top of the pot, and, when dry, the covering will be quite hard and air-tight.

Time.—½ to ¾ hour, reckoning from the time the jam boils all over.

Average cost, for a lb. pot, from 6d. to 8d.

Sufficient.—Allow from 6 to 7 quarts of currants to make 12 1-lb. pots of jam.

Seasonable.—Make this in July.

BAKED PEARS

Ingredients.—12 pears, the rind of 1 lemon, 6 cloves, 10 whole allspice: to every pint of water allow ½ lb. of loaf sugar.

Mode.—Pare and cut the pears into halves, and, should they be very large, into quarters; leave the stalks on, and carefully remove the cores. Place them in a clean baking-jar, with a closely-fitting lid; add to them the lemon-rind cut in strips, the juice of ½ lemon, the cloves, pounded allspice, and sufficient water just to cover the whole, with sugar in the above proportion. Cover the jar down closely, put it into a very cool oven, and bake the pears from 5 to 6 hours, but be very careful that the oven is not too hot. To improve the colour of the fruit, a few drops of prepared cochineal may be added; but this will not be found necessary if the pears are very gently baked.

Time.—Large pears, 5 to 6 hours, in a very slow oven.

Average cost.—1d. to 2d. each.

Sufficient for 7 or 8 persons.

Seasonable from September to January.

Pear.—The pear, like the apple, is indigenous to this country; but the wild pear is a very unsatisfactory fruit. The best varieties were brought from the East by the Romans, who cultivated them with care, and probably introduced some of their best sorts into this island, to which others were added by the inhabitants of the monasteries. The Dutch and Flemings, as well as the French, have excelled in the cultivation of the pear, and most of the late varieties introduced are from France and Flanders. The pear is a hardy tree, and a longer liver than the apple: it has been known to exist for centuries. There are now about 150 varieties of this fruit. Though perfectly wholesome when ripe, the pear is not so when green; but in this state it is fit for stewing. An agreeable beverage, called perry, is made from pears, and the varieties which are least fit for eating make the best perry.

PLUM JAM

Ingredients.—To every lb. of plums, weighed before being stoned, allow ¾ lb. of loaf sugar.

Mode.—In making plum jam, the quantity of sugar for each lb. of fruit must be regulated by the quality and size of the fruit, some plums requiring much more sugar than others. Divide the plums, take out the stones, and put them on to large dishes, with roughly-pounded sugar sprinkled over them in the above proportion, and let them remain for 1 day; then put them into a preserving-pan, stand them by the side of the fire to simmer gently for about ½ hour, and then boil them rapidly for another 15 minutes. The scum must be carefully removed as it rises, and the jam must be well stirred all the time, or it will burn at the bottom of the pan, and so spoil the colour and flavour of the preserve. Some of the stones may be cracked, and a few kernels added to the jam just before it is done: these impart a very delicious flavour to the plums. The above proportion of sugar would answer for Orleans plums; the Impératrice Magnum-bonum, and Winesour would not require quite so much.

Time.—½ hour to simmer gently, ¼ hour to boil rapidly.

Best plums for preserving.—Violets, Mussels, Orleans, Impératrice Magnum-bonum, and Winesour.

Seasonable from the end of July to the beginning of October.

Plums.—The Damson, or Damascene plum, takes its name from Damascus, where it grows in great quantities, and whence it was brought into Italy about 114 B.C. The Orleans plum is from France. The Greengage is called after the Gage family, who first brought it into England from the monastery of the Chartreuse, at Paris, where it still bears the name of Reine Claude. The Magnum-bonum is our largest plum, and greatly esteemed for preserves and culinary purposes. The best sorts of plums are agreeable at the dessert, and, when perfectly ripe, are wholesome; but some are too astringent. They lose much of their bad qualities by baking, and are extensively used, from their cheapness, when in full season, in tarts and preserves; but they are not a very wholesome fruit, and should be eaten in moderation.

SAGE-AND-ONION STUFFING

(For Geese, Ducks, and Pork)

Ingredients.—4 large onions, 10 sage-leaves, ¼ lb. of bread crumbs, 1½ oz. of butter, salt and pepper to taste, 1 egg.

Mode.—Peel the onions, put them into boiling water, let them simmer for 5 minutes or rather longer, and, just before they are taken out, put in the sage-leaves for a minute or 2 to take off their rawness. Chop both these very fine, add the bread, seasoning, and butter, and work the whole together with the yolk of an egg, when the stuffing will be ready for use. It should be rather highly seasoned, and the sage-leaves should be very finely chopped. Many cooks do not parboil the onions in the manner just stated, but merely use them raw. The stuffing then, however, is not nearly so mild, and, to many tastes, its strong flavour would be very objectionable. When made for goose, a portion of the liver of the bird, simmered for a few minutes and very finely minced, is frequently added to this stuffing; and where economy is studied, the egg may be dispensed with.

Time.—Rather more than 5 minutes to simmer the onions.

Average cost, for this quantity, 4d.

Sufficient for 1 goose, or a pair of ducks.

SALAD DRESSING

(*Excellent*)

Ingredients.—1 teaspoonful of mixed mustard, 1 teaspoonful of pounded sugar, 2 tablespoonfuls of salad-oil, 4 tablespoonfuls of milk, 2 tablespoonfuls of vinegar, cayenne and salt to taste.

Mode.—Put the mixed mustard into a salad-bowl with the sugar, and add the oil drop by drop, carefully stirring and mixing all these ingredients well together. Proceed in this manner with the milk and vinegar, which must be added very *gradually*, or the sauce will curdle. Put in the seasoning, when the mixture will be ready for use. If this dressing is properly made, it will have a soft creamy appearance, and will be found very delicious with crab, or cold fried fish (the latter cut into dice), as well as with salads. In mixing salad dressings, the ingredients cannot be added *too gradually*, or *stirred too much*.

Average cost, for this quantity, 3d.

Sufficient for a small salad.

Note.—This recipe can be confidently recommended by the editress, to whom it was given by an intimate friend noted for her salads.

APPLE SAUCE FOR GEESE, PORK, &c.

Ingredients.—6 good-sized apples, sifted sugar to taste, a piece of butter the size of a walnut, water.

Mode.—Pare, core, and quarter the apples, and throw them into cold water to preserve their whiteness. Put them in a saucepan, with sufficient water to moisten them, and boil till soft enough to pulp. Beat them up, adding sugar to taste, and a small piece of butter. This quantity is sufficient for a good-sized tureen.

Time.—According to the apples, about ¾ hour.

Average cost.—4d.

Sufficient, this quantity, for a goose or couple of ducks.

TOMATO SAUCE FOR KEEPING

(Excellent)

Ingredients.—To every quart of tomato-pulp allow 1 pint of cayenne vinegar, ¾ oz. of shalots, ¾ oz. of garlic, peeled and cut in slices; salt to taste. To every six quarts of liquor, 1 pint of soy, 1 pint of anchovy sauce.

Mode.—Gather the tomatoes quite ripe; bake them in a slow oven till tender; rub them through a sieve, and to every quart of pulp add cayenne vinegar, shalots, garlic, and salt, in the above proportion; boil the whole together till the garlic and shalots are quite soft; then rub it through a sieve, put it again into a saucepan, and, to every 6 quarts of the liquor, add 1 pint of soy and the same quantity of anchovy sauce, and boil altogether for about 20 minutes; bottle off for use, and carefully seal or rosin the corks. This will keep good for 2 or 3 years, but will be fit for use in a week. A useful and less expensive sauce may be made by omitting the anchovy and soy.

Time.—Altogether 1 hour.

Seasonable.—Make this from the middle of September to the end of October.

WALNUT KETCHUP

Ingredients.—100 walnuts, 1 handful of salt, 1 quart of vinegar, ¼ oz. of mace, ¼ oz. of nutmeg, ¼ oz. of cloves, ¼ oz. of ginger, ¼ oz. of whole black pepper, a small piece of horseradish, 20 shalots, ¼ lb. of anchovies, 1 pint of port wine.

Mode.—Procure the walnuts at the time you can run a pin through them, slightly bruise, and put them into a jar with the salt and vinegar, let them stand 8 days, stirring every day; then drain the liquor from them, and boil it, with the above ingredients, for about ½ hour. It may be strained or not, as preferred, and, if required, a little more vinegar or wine can be added, according to taste. When bottled well, seal the corks.

Time.—½ hour.

Seasonable.—Make this from the beginning to the middle of July, when walnuts are in perfection for pickling purposes.

THE WALNUT.

CHAPTER THIRTEEN

RECIPES FOR MAKING BREAD, BISCUITS, AND CAKES

ENGLISH AND FOREIGN LOAVES.

EXCELLENT ROLLS

Ingredients.—To every lb. of flour allow 1 oz. of butter, ¼ pint of milk, 1 large teaspoonful of yeast, a little salt.

ROLLS.

Mode.—Warm the butter in the milk, add to it the yeast and salt, and mix these ingredients well together. Put the flour into a pan, stir in the above ingredients, and let the dough rise, covered in a warm place. Knead it well, make it into rolls, let them rise again for a few minutes, and bake in a quick oven. Richer rolls may be made by adding 1 or 2 eggs and a larger proportion of butter, and their appearance improved by brushing the tops over with yolk of egg or a little milk

Time.—1 lb. of flour, divided into 6 rolls, from 15 to 20 minutes.

ALMOND CAKE

Ingredients.—½ lb. of sweet almonds, 1 oz. of bitter almonds, 6 eggs, 8 tablespoonfuls of sifted sugar, 5 tablespoonfuls of fine flour, the grated rind of 1 lemon, 3 oz. of butter.

Mode.—Blanch and pound the almonds to a paste; separate the whites from the yolks of the eggs; beat the latter, and add them to the almonds. Stir in the sugar, flour, and lemon-rind; add the butter, which should be beaten to a cream; and when all these ingredients are well mixed, put in the whites of the eggs, which should be whisked to a stiff froth. Butter a cake-mould, put in the mixture, and bake in a good oven from 1¼ to 1¾ hour.

Time.—1¼ to 1¾ hour.

Average cost.—1s.

Seasonable at any time.

HOLIDAY CAKE

Ingredients.—1½d. worth of Borwick's German baking-powder, 2 lbs. of flour, 6 oz. of butter, ¼ lb. of lard, 1 lb. of currants, ½ lb. of stoned and cut raisins, ¼ lb. of mixed candied peel, ½ lb. of moist sugar, 3 eggs, ¾ pint of cold milk.

Mode.—Mix the baking-powder with the flour; then rub in the butter and lard; have ready the currants, washed, picked, and dried, the raisins stoned and cut into small pieces (not chopped), and the peel cut into neat slices. Add these with the sugar to the flour, &c., and mix all the dry ingredients well together. Whisk the eggs, stir to them the milk, and with this liquid moisten the cake; beat it up well, that all may be very thoroughly mixed; line a cake-tin with buttered paper, put in the cake, and bake it from 2¼ to 2¾ hours in a good oven. To ascertain when it is done, plunge a clean knife into the middle of it, and if, on withdrawing it, the knife looks clean, and not sticky, the cake is done. To prevent its burning at the top, a piece of clean paper may be put over whilst the cake is soaking, or being thoroughly cooked in the middle. A steamer, such as is used for steaming potatoes, makes a very good cake-tin, if it be lined at the bottom and sides with buttered paper.

Time.—2¼ to 2¾ hours.

Average cost.—2s. 6d.

Seasonable at any time.

LEMON CAKE

Ingredients.—10 eggs, 3 tablespoonfuls of orange-flower water, ¾ lb. of pounded loaf sugar, 1 lemon, ¾ lb. of flour.

Mode.—Separate the whites from the yolks of the eggs; whisk the former to a stiff froth; add the orange-flower water, the sugar, grated lemon-rind, and mix these ingredients well together. Then beat the yolks of the eggs, and add them, with the lemon-juice, to the whites, &c.; dredge in the flour gradually; keep beating the mixture well; put it into a buttered mould, and bake the cake about an hour, or rather longer. The addition of a little butter, beaten to a cream, we think, would improve this cake.

Time.—About 1 hour.

Average cost.—1s. 4d.

Seasonable at any time.

CAKE-MOULD.

CHAPTER FOURTEEN

RECIPES FOR BEVERAGES

TEA, COFFEE, &c.

TO MAKE TEA

There is very little art in making good tea; if the water is boiling, and there is no sparing of the fragrant leaf, the beverage will almost invariably be good. The old-fashioned plan of allowing a teaspoonful to each person, and 1 over, is still practised. Warm the teapot with boiling water; let it remain for 2 or 3 minutes for the vessel to become thoroughly hot, then pour it away. Put in the tea, pour in from ½ to ¾ pint of boiling water, close the lid, and let it stand for the tea to draw from 5 to 10 minutes; then fill up the pot with water. The tea will be quite spoiled unless made with water that is actually 'boiling', as the leaves will not open, and the flavour not be extracted from them; the beverage will consequently be colourless and tasteless,—in fact, nothing but tepid water. Where there is a very large party to make tea for, it is a good plan to have 2 teapots instead of putting a large quantity of tea into 1 pot; the tea, besides, will go farther. When the infusion has been once completed, the addition of fresh tea adds very little to the strength; so when more is required, have the pot emptied of the old leaves, scalded, and fresh tea made in the usual manner. Economists say that a few grains of carbonate of soda, added before the boiling water is poured on the tea, assist to draw out the goodness: if the water is very hard, perhaps it is a good plan, as the soda softens it; but care must be taken to use this ingredient sparingly, as it is liable to give the tea a soapy taste if added in too large a quantity. For mixed tea, the usual proportion is 4 spoonfuls of black to 1 of green; more of the latter when the flavour is very much liked; but strong green tea is highly pernicious, and should never be partaken of too freely.

Time.—2 minutes to warm the teapot, 5 to 10 minutes to draw the strength from the tea.

Sufficient.—Allow 1 teaspoonful to each person, and 1 over.

Tea.—The tea-tree or shrub belongs to the class and order of Monadelphia polyandria in the Linnaean system, and to the natural order of Aurantiaceae in the system of Jussieu. Lately it has been made into a new order, the Theasia, which includes the Camellia and some other plants. It commonly grows to the height of from three to six feet; but it is said, that, in its wild or native state, it reaches twenty feet or more. In China it is cultivated in numerous small plantations. In its general appearance, and the form of its leaf, it resembles the myrtle. The blossoms are white and fragrant, not unlike those of the wild rose, but smaller; and they are succeeded by soft green capsules, containing each from one to three white seeds. These capsules are crushed for oil, which is in general use in China.

GINGER WINE

Ingredients.—To 9 gallons of water allow 27 lbs. of loaf sugar, 9 lemons, 12 oz. of bruised ginger, 3 tablespoonfuls of yeast, 2 lbs. of raisins stoned and chopped, 1 pint of brandy.

Mode.—Boil together for 1 hour in a copper (let it previously be well scoured and beautifully clean) the water, sugar, *lemon-rinds*, and bruised ginger; remove every particle of scum as it rises, and when the liquor is sufficiently boiled, put it into a large tub or pan, as it must not remain in the copper. When nearly cold, add the yeast, which must be thick and very fresh, and, the next day, put all in a dry cask with the strained lemon-juice and chopped raisins. Stir the wine every day for a fortnight; then add the brandy, stop the cask down by degrees, and in a few weeks it will be fit to bottle.

Average cost.—2s. per gallon.

Sufficient to make 9 gallons of wine.

Seasonable.—The best time for making this wine is either in March or September.

Note.—Wine made early in March will be fit to bottle in June.

CHAMPAGNE CUP

Ingredients.—1 quart bottle of champagne, 2 bottles of soda-water, 1 liqueur-glass of brandy or Curaçoa, 2 tablespoonfuls of powdered sugar, 1 lb. of pounded ice, a sprig of green borage.

Mode.—Put all the ingredients into a silver cup; stir them together, and serve. Should the above proportion of sugar not be found sufficient to suit some tastes, increase the quantity. When borage is not easily obtainable, substitute for it a few slices of cucumber-rind.

Seasonable.—Suitable for pic-nics, balls, weddings, and other festive occasions.

Champagne.—This, the most celebrated of French wines, is the produce chiefly of the province of that name, and is generally understood in England to be a brisk, effervescing, or sparkling white wine, of a very fine flavour; but this is only one of the varieties of this class. There is both red and white champagne, and each of these may be either still or brisk. There are the sparkling wines (mousseux), and the still wines (non-mousseux). The brisk are in general the most highly esteemed, or, at least, are the most popular in this country, on account of their delicate flavour and the agreeable pungency which they derive from the carbonic acid they contain, and to which they owe their briskness.

CLARET CUP

Ingredients.—1 bottle of claret, 1 bottle of soda-water, about ½ lb. of pounded ice, 4 tablespoonfuls of powdered sugar, ¼ teaspoonful of grated nutmeg, 1 liqueur-glass of Maraschino, a sprig of green borage.

Mode.—Put all the ingredients into a silver cup, regulating the proportion of ice by the state of the weather: if very warm, a larger quantity would be necessary. Hand the cup round with a clean napkin passed through one of the handles, that the edge of the cup may be wiped after each guest has partaken of the contents thereof.

Seasonable in summer.

Clarets.—All those wines called in England clarets are the produce of the country round Bordeaux, or the Bordelais; but it is remarkable that there is no pure wine in France known by the name of claret, which is a corruption of *clairet*, a term that is applied there to any red or rose-coloured wine. Round Bordeaux are produced a number of wines of the first quality, which pass under the name simply of *vins de Bordeaux*, or have the designation of the particular district where they are made; as Lafitte, Latour, &c. The clarets brought to the English market are frequently prepared for it by the wine-growers by mixing together several Bordeaux wines, or by adding to them a portion of some other wines; but in France the pure wines are carefully preserved distinct. The genuine wines of Bordeaux are of great variety, that part being one of the most distinguished in France; and the principal vineyards are

those of Medoc, Palus, Graves, and Blanche, the product
of each having characters considerably different.

GINGER BEER

Ingredients.—2½ lbs. of loaf sugar, 1½ oz. of bruised ginger, 1 oz. of cream of tartar, the rind and juice of 2 lemons, 3 gallons of boiling water, 2 large tablespoonfuls of thick and fresh brewer's yeast.

Mode.—Peel the lemons, squeeze the juice, strain it, and put the peel and juice into a large earthen pan, with the bruised ginger, cream of tartar, and loaf sugar. Pour over these ingredients 3 gallons of boiling water; let it stand until just warm, when add the yeast, which should be thick and perfectly fresh. Stir the contents of the pan well, and let them remain near the fire all night, covering the pan over with a cloth. The next day skim off the yeast, and pour the liquor carefully into another vessel, leaving the sediment; then bottle immediately, and tie the corks down, and in 3 days the ginger beer will be fit for use. For some tastes, the above proportion of sugar may be found rather too large, when it may be diminished; but the beer will not keep so long good.

Average cost for this quantity, 2s.; or ½d. per bottle.

Sufficient to fill 4 dozen ginger-beer bottles.

Seasonable.—This should be made during the summer months.

LEMONADE

Ingredients.—The rind of 2 lemons, the juice of 3 large or 4 small ones, 1 lb. of loaf sugar, 1 quart of boiling water.

Mode.—Rub some of the sugar, in lumps, on 2 of the lemons until they have imbibed all the oil from them, and put it with the remainder of the sugar into a jug; add the lemon-juice (but no pips), and pour over the whole a quart of boiling water. When the sugar is dissolved, strain the lemonade through a fine sieve or piece of muslin, and, when cool, it will be ready for use. The lemonade will be much improved by having the white of an egg beaten up in it; a little sherry mixed with it, also, makes this beverage much nicer.

Average cost.—6d. per quart.

TO MULL WINE

Ingredients.—To every pint of wine allow 1 large cupful of water, sugar and spice to taste.

Mode.—In making preparations like the above, it is very difficult to give the exact proportions of ingredients like sugar and spice, as what quantity might suit one person would be to another quite distasteful. Boil the spice in the water until the flavour is extracted, then add the wine and sugar, and bring the whole to the boiling-point, when serve with strips of crisp dry toast, or with biscuits. The spices usually used for mulled wine are cloves, grated nutmeg, and cinnamon or mace. Any kind of wine may be mulled, but port and claret are those usually selected for the purpose; and the latter requires a very large proportion of sugar. The vessel that the wine is boiled in must be delicately clean, and should be kept exclusively for the purpose. Small tin warmers may be purchased for a trifle, which are more suitable than saucepans, as, if the latter are not scrupulously clean, they will spoil the wine, by imparting to it a very disagreeable flavour. These warmers should be used for no other purposes.

MULL.

TO MAKE HOT PUNCH

Ingredients.—½ pint of rum, ½ pint of brandy, ¼ lb. of sugar, 1 large lemon, ½ teaspoonful of nutmeg, 1 pint of boiling water.

Mode.—Rub the sugar over the lemon until it has absorbed all the yellow part of the skin, then put the sugar into a punchbowl; add the lemon-juice (free from pips), and mix these two ingredients well together. Pour over them the boiling water, stir well together, add the rum, brandy, and nutmeg; mix thoroughly, and the punch will be ready to serve. It is very important in making good punch that all the ingredients are thoroughly incorporated; and, to insure success, the processes of mixing must be diligently attended to.

Sufficient.—Allow a quart for 4 persons; but this information must be taken *cum grano salis*; for the capacities of persons for this kind of beverage are generally supposed to vary considerably.

Punch is a beverage made of various spirituous liquors or wine, hot water, the acid juice of fruits, and sugar. It is considered to be very intoxicating; but this is probably because the spirit, being partly sheathed by the mucilaginous juice and the sugar, its strength does not appear to the taste so great as it really is. Punch, which was almost universally drunk among the middle classes about fifty or sixty years ago, has almost disappeared from our domestic tables, being superseded by wine. There are many different varieties of punch. It is sometimes kept cold in bottles, and makes a most agreeable summer drink. In Scotland, instead of the Madeira or sherry generally used in its manufacture, whiskey is substituted, and then its insidious properties are more than usually felt. Where fresh lemons cannot be had for punch or similar beverages, crystallized citric acid and a few drops of the essence of lemon will be very nearly the same thing. In the composition of "Regent's punch," champagne, brandy, and *veritable Martinique* are required; "Norfolk punch" requires Seville oranges; "Milk punch" may be extemporised by adding a little hot milk to lemonade, and then straining it through a jelly-bag. Then there are "Wine punch," "Tea punch," and "French punch," made with lemons, spirits, and wine, in fantastic proportions. But of all the compounds of these materials, perhaps, for a *summer* drink, the North–American "mint julep" is the most inviting. Captain Marryat gives the following recipe for its preparation:—"Put into a tumbler about a dozen sprigs of the tender shoots of mint; upon them put a spoonful of white sugar, and equal proportions of peach and common brandy, so as to fill up one-third, or, perhaps, a little less; then take rasped or pounded ice, and fill up the tumbler. Epicures rub the lips of the tumbler with a piece of fresh pineapple; and the tumbler itself is very often encrusted outside with stalactites of ice. As the ice melts, you drink." The Virginians, say Captain Marryat, claim the merit of having invented this superb compound; but, from a passage in the "Comus" of Milton, he claims it for his own country.

WHISKEY CORDIAL

Ingredients.—1 lb. of ripe white currants, the rind of 2 lemons, ¼ oz. of grated ginger, 1 quart of whiskey, 1 lb. of lump sugar.

Mode.—Strip the currants from the stalks; put them into a large jug; add the lemon-rind, ginger, and whiskey; cover the jug closely, and let it remain covered for 24 hours. Strain through a hair sieve, add the lump sugar, and let it stand 12 hours longer; then bottle, and cork well.

Time.—To stand 24 hours before being strained; 12 hours after the sugar is added.

Seasonable.—Make this in July.

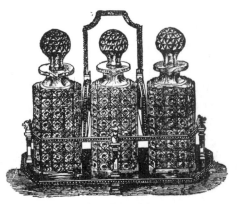

SPIRIT STAND.

258

CHAPTER FIFTEEN

RECIPES FOR INVALID COOKERY

BARLEY GRUEL

Ingredients.—2 oz. of Scotch or pearl barley, ½ pint of port wine, the rind of 1 lemon, 1 quart and ½ pint of water, sugar to taste.

Mode.—After well washing the barley, boil it in ½ pint of water for ¼ hour; then pour this water away; put to the barley the quart of fresh boiling water, and let it boil until the liquid is reduced to half; then strain it off. Add the wine, sugar, and lemon-peel; simmer for 5 minutes, and put it away in a clean jug. It can be warmed from time to time, as required.

Time.—To be boiled until reduced to half.

Average cost.—1s. 6d.

Sufficient with the wine to make 1½ pint of gruel.

TO MAKE BEEF TEA

Ingredients.—1 lb. of lean gravy-beef, 1 quart of water, 1 saltspoonful of salt.

Mode.—Have the meat cut without fat and bone, and choose a nice fleshy piece. Cut it into small pieces about the size of dice, and put it into a clean saucepan. Add the water *cold* to it; put it on the fire, and bring it to the boiling-point; then skim well. Put in the salt when the water boils, and *simmer* the beef tea *gently* from ½ to ¾ hour, removing any more scum should it appear on the surface. Strain the tea through a hair sieve, and set it by in a cool place. When wanted for use, remove every particle of fat from the top; warm up as much as may be required, adding, if necessary, a little more salt. This preparation is simple beef tea, and is to be administered to those invalids to whom flavourings and seasonings are not allowed. When the patient is very low, use double the quantity of meat to the same proportion of water. Should the invalid be able to take the tea prepared in a more palatable manner, it is easy to make it so by following the directions in the next recipe, which is an admirable one for making savoury beef tea. Beef tea is always better when made the day before it is wanted, and then warmed up. It is a good plan to put the tea into a small cup or basin, and to place this basin in a saucepan of boiling water. When the tea is warm, it is ready to serve.

Time.—¼ to ¾ hour.

Average cost.—6d. per pint.

Sufficient.—Allow 1 lb. of meat for a pint of good beef tea.

MISS NIGHTINGALE says, one of the most common errors among nurses, with respect to sick diet, is the belief that beef tea is the most nutritive of all article. She says, "Just try and boil down a lb. of beef into beef tea; evaporate your beef tea, and see what is left of your beef: you will find that there is barely a teaspoonful of solid nourishment to ¼ pint of water in beef tea. Nevertheless, there is a certain reparative quality in it,—we do not know what,—as there is in tea; but it may be safely given in almost any inflammatory disease, and is as little to be depended upon with the healthy or convalescent, where much nourishment is required."

CALF'S-FOOT BROTH

Ingredients.—1 calf's foot, 3 pints of water, 1 small lump of sugar, nutmeg to taste, the yolk of 1 egg, a piece of butter the size of a nut.

Mode.—Stew the foot in the water, with the lemon-peel, very gently, until the liquid is half wasted, removing any scum, should it rise to the surface. Set it by in a basin until quite cold, then take off every particle of fat. Warm up about ½ pint of the broth, adding the butter, sugar, and a very small quantity of grated nutmeg; take it off the fire for a minute or 2, then add the beaten yolk of the egg; keep stirring over the fire until the mixture thickens, but do not allow it to boil again after the egg is added, or it will curdle, and the broth will be spoiled.

Time.—To be boiled until the liquid is reduced one half.

Average cost, in full season, 9d. each.

Sufficient to make 1¼ pint of broth.

Seasonable from March to October.

CHICKEN BROTH

Ingredients.—½ fowl, or the inferior joints of a whole one; 1 quart of water, 1 blade of mace, ½ onion, a small bunch of sweet herbs, salt to taste, 10 peppercorns.

Mode.—An old fowl not suitable for eating may be converted into very good broth, or, if a young one be used, the inferior joints may be put in the broth, and the best pieces reserved for dressing in some other manner. Put the fowl into a saucepan, with all the ingredients, and simmer gently for 1½ hour, carefully skimming the broth well. When done, strain, and put by in a cool place until wanted; then take all the fat off the top, warm up as much as may be required, and serve. This broth is, of course, only for those invalids whose stomachs are strong enough to digest it, with a flavouring of herbs, &c. It may be made in the same manner as beef tea, with water and salt only; but the preparation will be but tasteless and insipid. When the invalid cannot digest this chicken broth with the flavouring, we would recommend plain beef tea in preference to plain chicken tea, which it would be without the addition of herbs, onions, &c.

Time.—1½ hour.

Sufficient to make rather more than 1 pint of broth.

EEL BROTH

Ingredients.—½ lb. of eels, a small bunch of sweet herbs, including parsley; ½ onion, 10 peppercorns, 3 pints of water, 2 cloves, salt and pepper to taste.

Mode.—After having cleaned and skinned the eel, cut it into small pieces, and put it into a stewpan, with the other ingredients; simmer gently until the liquid is reduced nearly half, carefully removing the scum as it rises. Strain it through a hair sieve; put it by in a cool place, and, when wanted, take off all the fat from the top, warm up as much as is required, and serve with sippets of toasted bread. This is a very nutritious broth, and easy of digestion.

Time.—To be simmered until the liquor is reduced to half.

Average cost.—6d.

Sufficient to make 1½ pint of broth.

Seasonable from June to March.

HOUSEHOLD
MANAGEMENT

CHAPTER SIXTEEN

DOMESTIC SERVANTS

GENERAL OBSERVATIONS ON DOMESTIC SERVANTS

IT IS THE CUSTOM OF "SOCIETY" to abuse its servants,—*à façon de parler*, such as leads their lords and masters to talk of the weather, and, when rurally inclined, of the crops,—leads matronly ladies, and ladies just entering on their probation in that honoured and honourable state, to talk of servants, and, as we are told, wax eloquent over the greatest plague in life while taking a quiet cup of tea. Young men at their clubs, also, we are told, like to abuse their "fellows," perhaps not without a certain pride and pleasure at the opportunity of intimating that they enjoy such appendages to their state. It is another conviction of "Society" that the race of good servants has died out, at least in England, although they do order these things better in France; that there is neither honesty, conscientiousness, nor the careful and industrious habits which distinguished the servants of our grandmothers and great-grandmothers; that domestics no longer know their place; that the introduction of cheap silks and cottons, and, still more recently, those ambiguous "materials" and tweeds, have removed the landmarks between the mistress and her maid, between the master and his man.

Choice of Servants.—When the distinction really depends on things so insignificant, this is very probably the case; when the lady of fashion chooses her footman without any other consideration than his height, shape, and *tournure* of his calf, it is not surprising that she should find a domestic who has no attachment for the family, who considers the figure he cuts behind her carriage, and the late hours he is compelled to keep, a full compensation for the wages he exacts, for the food he wastes, and for the perquisites he can lay his hands on. Nor should the fast young man, who chooses his groom for his knowingness in the ways of the turf and in the tricks of low horse-dealers, be surprised if he is sometimes the victim of these learned ways. But these are the exceptional cases, which prove the existence of a better state of things. The great masses of society among us are not thus deserted; there are few families of respectability, from the shopkeeper in the next street to the nobleman whose mansion dignifies the next square, which do not contain among their dependents attached and useful servants; and where these are absent altogether, there are good reasons for it.

Masters and Mistresses.—It has been said that good masters and mistresses make good servants, and this to a great extent is true. There are certainly some men and women in the wide field of servitude whom it would be impossible to train into good servants, but the conduct of both master and mistress is seldom without its effect upon these dependents.

They are not mere machines, and no one has a right to consider them in that light. The sensible master and the kind mistress know, that if servants depend on them for their means of living, in their turn they are dependent on their servants for very many of the comforts of life; and that, with a proper amount of care in choosing servants, and treating them like reasonable beings, and making slight excuses for the shortcomings of human nature, they will, save in some exceptional case, be tolerably well served, and, in most instances, surround themselves with attached domestics.

This remark, which is applicable to all domestics, is especially so to men-servants. Families accustomed to such attendants have always about them humble dependents, whose children have no other prospect than domestic service to look forward to; to them it presents no degradation, but the reverse, to be so employed; they are initiated step by step into the mysteries of the household, with the prospect of rising in the service, if it is a house admitting of promotion,—to the respectable position of butler or house-steward. In families of humbler pretensions, where they must look for promotion elsewhere, they know that can only be attained by acquiring the goodwill of their employers. Can there be any stronger security for their good conduct,—any doubt that, in the mass of domestic servants, good conduct is the rule, the reverse the exception?

DUTIES OF THE BUTLER

The domestic duties of the butler are to bring in the eatables at breakfast, and wait upon the family at that meal, assisted by the footman, and see to the cleanliness of everything at table. On taking away, he removes the tray with the china and plate, for which he is responsible. At luncheon, he arranges the meal, and waits unassisted, the footman being now engaged in other duties. At dinner, he places the silver and plated articles on the table, sees that everything is in its place, and rectifies what is wrong. He carries in the first dish, and announces in the drawing-room that dinner is on the table, and respectfully stands by the door until the company are seated, when he takes his place behind his master's chair on the left, to remove the covers, handing them to the other attendants to carry out. After the first course of plates is supplied, his place is at the sideboard to serve the wines, but only when called on. The first course ended, he rings the cook's bell, and hands the dishes from the table to the other servants to carry away, receiving from them the second course, which he places on the table, removing the covers as before, and again taking his place at the sideboard.

Before dinner he has satisfied himself that the lamps, candles, or gas-burners are in perfect order, if not lighted, which will usually be the case.

Carving at dinner is now generally done by the butler, for even the every-day family dinner is not put upon the table, the chief man-servant carving each dish at a side table. After serving the soups the butler has time to pour out the sherry or Madeira taken after that course, then he returns to his post at the side table. Where there is much to be carved a helper is sometimes needed, but entrées have now so superseded the old-fashioned joints, that a skilful carver can easily manage to do all that is necessary even at a large dinner.

After dinner the butler receives the dessert from the other servants, and arranges it on the table, with plates and glasses, and then takes his place behind his master's chair to hand the wines and ices, while the footman stands behind his mistress for the same purpose, the other attendants leaving the room. Where the old-fashioned practice of having the dessert on the polished table, without any cloth, is still adhered to, the butler should rub off any marks made by the hot dishes before arranging the dessert. Having served every one with their share of the dessert, put the fires in order (when these are used), and seen the lights are all right, at a signal from his master, he and the footman leave the room.

He now proceeds to the drawing-room, arranges the fireplace, and sees to the lights; he then returns to his pantry, prepared to answer the bell, and attend to the company, while the footman is clearing away and cleaning the plate and glasses.

At tea he again attends. At bedtime he appears with the candles; he locks up the plate, secures doors and windows, and sees that all the fires are safe.

In addition to these duties, the butler, where only one footman is kept, will be required to perform some of the duties of the valet, to pay bills, and superintend the other servants. But the real duties of the butler are in the wine-cellar; there he should be competent to advise his master as to the price and quality of the wine to be laid in; "fine," bottle, cork, and seal it, and place it in the binns. Brewing, racking, and bottling malt liquors, belong to his office, as well as their distribution. These and other drinkables are brought from the cellar every day by his own hands, except where an under-butler is kept; and a careful entry of every bottle used, entered in the cellar-book; so that the book should always show the contents of the cellar.

The butler should make it his business to understand the proper treatment of the different wines under his charge, which he can easily do from the wine-merchant, and faithfully attend to it; his own reputation will soon compensate for the absence of bribes from unprincipled wine-merchants, if he serves a generous and hospitable master. Nothing spreads more rapidly in society than the reputation of a good wine-cellar, and all that is required is wines well chosen and well cared for; and this a little knowledge, carefully applied, will soon supply.

Having charge of the contents of the cellars, it is the butler's duty to keep them in a proper condition, to fine down wine in wood, bottle it off, and store it away in places suited to the sorts. Where wine comes into the cellar ready bottled, it is usual to return the same number of empty bottles; the butler has not, in this case, the same inducements to keep the bottles of the different sorts separated; but where the wine is bottled in the house, he will find his account, not only in keeping them separate, but in rinsing them well, and even washing them with clean water as soon as they are empty.

THE BUTLER.

DUTIES OF THE FOOTMAN

Where a single footman, or odd man, is the only male servant, then, whatever his ostensible position, he is required to make himself generally useful. He has to clean the knives and shoes, the furniture, the plate; answer the visitors who call, the drawing-room and parlour bells; and do all the errands. His life is no sinecure; and a methodical arrangement of his time will be necessary, in order to perform his many duties with any satisfaction to himself or his master.

The footman only finds himself in stockings, shoes, and washing. Where silk stockings, or other extra articles of linen are worn, they are found by the family, as well as his livery, a working dress, consisting of a pair of overalls, a waistcoat, a fustian jacket, with a white or jean one for times when he is liable to be called to answer the door or wait at breakfast; and, on quitting his service, he is expected to leave behind him any livery had within six months.

The footman is expected to rise early, in order to get through all his dirty work before the family are stirring. Boots and shoes, and knives and forks, should be cleaned, lamps in use trimmed, his master's clothes brushed, the furniture rubbed over; so that he may put aside his working dress, tidy himself, and appear in a clean jean jacket to lay the cloth and prepare breakfast for the family.

We need hardly dwell on the boot-cleaning process: three good brushes and good blacking must be provided; one of the brushes hard, to brush off the mud; the other soft, to lay on the blacking; the third of a medium hardness, for polishing; and each should be kept for its particular use. The blacking should be kept corked up, except when in use, and applied to the brush with a sponge tied to a stick, which, when put away, rests in a notch cut in the cork. When boots come in very muddy, it is a good practice to wash off the mud, and wipe them dry with a sponge; then leave them to dry very gradually on their sides, taking care they are not placed near the fire, or scorched. Much delicacy of treatment is required in cleaning ladies' boots, so as to make the leather look well-polished, and the upper part retain a fresh appearance, with the lining free from hand-marks, which are very offensive to a lady of refined tastes.

Patent leather boots require to be wiped with a wet sponge, and afterwards with a soft dry cloth, and occasionally with a soft cloth and sweet oil, blacking and polishing the edge of the soles in the usual way, but so as not to cover the patent polish with blacking. A little milk may also be used with very good effect for patent leather boots.

Top boots are still occasionally worn by gentlemen. While cleaning the lower part in the usual manner, protect the tops, by inserting a cloth or brown paper under the edges and bringing it over them. In cleaning the tops, let the covering fall down over the boot; wash the tops clean with soap and flannel, and rub out any spots with pumice-stone. If the tops are to be whiter, dissolve an ounce of oxalic acid and half an ounce of pumice-stone in a pint of soft water; if a brown colour is intended, mix an ounce of muriatic acid, half an ounce of alum, half an ounce of gum Arabic, and half an ounce of spirit of lavender, in a pint and a half of skimmed milk "turned." These mixtures apply by means of a sponge, and polish, when dry, with a rubber made of soft flannel.

Knives are now generally cleaned by means of Kent's or Masters's machine, which gives very little trouble, and is very effective; before, however, putting the knives into the machine, it is highly necessary that they be first washed in a little warm (not hot) water, and then thoroughly wiped: if put into the machine with any grease on them, it adheres to the brushes, and consequently renders them unfit to use for the next knives that may be put in. When this precaution is not taken, the machine must come to pieces, so causing an immense amount of trouble, which may all be avoided by having the knives thoroughly free from grease before using the machine. Brushes are also used for cleaning forks, which facilitate the operation. When knives are so cleaned, see that they are carefully polished, wiped, and with a good edge, the ferules and prongs free from dirt, and place them in the basket with the handles all one way.

Lamp-trimming requires a thorough acquaintance with the mechanism; after that, constant attention to cleanliness, and an occasional entire clearing out with hot water: when this is done, all the parts should be carefully dried before filling again with oil. When lacquered, wipe the lacquered parts with a soft brush and cloth, and wash occasionally with weak soapsuds, wiping carefully afterwards. Brass lamps may be cleaned with oil and rottenstone every day when trimmed. With bronze, and other ornamental lamps, more care will be required, and soft flannel and oil only used, to prevent the removal of the bronze or enamel. Brass-work, or any metal-work not lacquered, is cleaned by a little oil and rottenstone made into a paste, or with fine emery-powder and oil mixed in the same manner. A small portion of sal-ammoniac, beat into a fine powder and moistened with soft water, rubbed over brass ornaments, and heated over a charcoal fire, and rubbed dry with bran or whitening, will give to brass-work the brilliancy of gold. In trimming moderator lamps, let the wick be cut evenly all round; as, if left higher in one place than it is in another, it will cause it to smoke and burn badly. The lamp should then be filled with oil from a feeder, and afterwards well wiped with a cloth or rag kept for the purpose. If it can be avoided, never wash the chimneys of a lamp, as it causes them to crack when they become hot. Small sticks, covered with wash-leather pads, are the best things to use for cleaning the glasses inside, and a clean duster for polishing the outside. The globe of a moderator lamp should be occasionally washed in warm soap-and-water, then well rinsed in cold water, and either wiped dry or left to drain. Where candle-lamps are used, take out the springs occasionally, and free them well from the grease that adheres to them.

French polish, so universally applied to furniture, is easily kept in condition by dusting and rubbing with a soft cloth, or a rubber of old silk; but dining-tables can only be kept in order by hard rubbing, or rather by quick rubbing, which warms the wood and removes all spots.

Brushing clothes is a very simple but very necessary operation. Fine cloths require to be brushed lightly, and with rather a soft brush, except where mud is to be removed, when a hard one is necessary, being previously beaten lightly to dislodge the dirt. Lay the garment on a table, and brush it in the direction of the nap. Having brushed it properly, turn the sleeves back to the collar, so that the folds may come at the elbow-joints; next turn the lappels or sides back over the folded sleeves; then lay the skirts over level with the collar, so that the crease may fall about the centre, and double one half over the other, so as the fold comes in the centre of the back.

Having got through his dirty work, the single footman has now to clean himself and prepare the breakfast. He lays the cloth on the table; over it the breakfast-cloth, and sets the breakfast things in order, and then proceeds to wait upon his master, if he has any of the duties of a valet to perform.

Where a valet is not kept, a portion of his duties falls to the footman's share,—brushing the clothes among others. When the hat is silk, it requires brushing every day with a soft brush; after rain, it requires wiping the way of the nap before drying, and, when nearly dry, brushing with the soft brush and with the hat-stick in it. If the footman is required to perform any part of a valet's duties, he will have to see that the housemaid lights a fire in the dressing-room in due time; that the room is dusted and cleaned; that the washhand-ewer is filled with soft water; and that the bath, whether hot or cold, is ready when required; that towels are at hand; that hair-brushes and combs are properly cleansed, and in their places; that hot water is ready at the hour ordered; the dressing-gown and slippers in their place, the clean linen aired, and the clothes to be worn for the day in their proper places. After the master has dressed, it will be the footman's duty to restore everything to its place properly cleansed and dry, and the whole restored to order.

At breakfast, when there is no butler, the footman carries up the tea-urn, and, assisted by the housemaid, he waits during breakfast. Breakfast over, he removes the tray and other things off the table, folds up the breakfast-cloth, and sets the room in order, by sweeping up all crumbs, shaking the cloth, and laying it on the table again, making up the fire, and sweeping up the hearth.

At luncheon-time nearly the same routine is observed, except where the footman is either out with the carriage or away on other business, when, in the absence of any butler, the housemaid must assist.

For dinner, the footman lays the cloth, taking care that the table is not too near the fire, if there is one, and that passage-room is left. A tablecloth should be laid without a wrinkle; and this requires two persons: over this the slips are laid, which are usually removed preparatory to placing dessert on the table. He prepares knives, forks, and glasses, with five or six plates for each person. This done, he places chairs enough for the party, distributing them equally on each side of the table, and opposite to each a napkin neatly folded, within it a piece of bread or small roll, and a knife on the right side of each plate, a fork on the left, and a carving-knife and fork at the top and bottom of the table, outside the others, with the rests opposite to them, and a gravy-spoon beside the knife.

The fish-slice should be at the top, where the lady of the house, with the assistance of the gentleman next to her, divides the fish, and the soup-ladle at the bottom: it is sometimes usual to add a dessert-knife and fork; at the same time, on the right side also of each plate, put a wine-glass for as many kinds of wine as it is intended to hand round, and a finger-glass or glass-cooler about four inches from the edge. The latter are frequently put on the table with the dessert.

About half an hour before dinner, he rings the dinner-bell, where that is the practice, and occupies himself with carrying up everything he is likely to require. At the expiration of the time, having communicated with the cook, he rings the real dinner-bell, and proceeds to take it up with such assistance as he can obtain. Having ascertained that all is in order, that his own dress is clean and presentable, and his white cotton gloves are without a stain, he announces in the drawing-room that dinner is served, and stands respectfully by the door until the company are seated: he places himself on the left, behind his master who is to distribute the soup; where soup and fish are served together, his place will be at his mistress's left hand; but he must be on the alert to see that whoever is assisting him, whether male or female, are at their posts. If any of the guests has brought his own servant with him, his place is behind his master's chair, rendering such assistance to others as he can, while attending to his master's wants throughout the dinner, so that every guest has what he requires. This necessitates both activity and intelligence, and should be done without bustle, without asking any questions, except where it is the custom of the house to hand round dishes or wine, when it will be necessary to mention, in a quiet and unobtrusive manner, the dish or wine you present.

Salt-cellars should be placed on the table in number sufficient for the guests, so that each may help themselves, or, at least, their immediate neighbours.

THE FOOTMAN.

DUTIES OF THE HOUSEMAID

"Cleanliness is next to godliness," saith the proverb, and "order" is in the next degree; the housemaid, then, may be said to be the handmaiden to two of the most prominent virtues. Her duties are very numerous, and many of the comforts of the family depend on their performance; but they are simple and easy to a person naturally clean and orderly, and desirous of giving satisfaction. In all families, whatever the habits of the master and mistress, servants will find it advantageous to rise early; their daily work will thus come easy to them. If they rise late, there is a struggle to overtake it, which throws an air of haste and hurry over the whole establishment. Where the master's time is regulated by early business or professional engagements, this will, of course, regulate the hours of the servants; but even where that is not the case, servants will find great personal convenience in rising early and getting through their work in an orderly and methodical manner. The housemaid who studies her own ease will certainly be at her work by six o'clock in the summer, and, probably, half-past six or seven in the winter months, having spent a reasonable time in her own chamber in dressing. Earlier than this would, probably, be an unnecessary waste of coals and candle in winter.

The first duty of the housemaid in winter is to open the shutters of all the lower rooms in the house, and take up the hearth-rugs of those rooms which she is going to "do" before breakfast. In some families, where there is only a cook and housemaid kept, and where the drawing-rooms are large, the cook has the care of the dining-room, and the housemaid that of the breakfast-room, library, and drawing-rooms. After the shutters are all opened, she sweeps the breakfast-room, sweeping the dust towards the fire-place, of course previously removing the fonder. She should then lay a cloth (generally made of coarse wrappering) over the carpet in front of the stove, and on this should place her housemaid's box, containing black-lead brushes, leathers, emery-paper, cloth, black lead, and all utensils necessary for cleaning a grate, with the cinder-pail on the other side. She now sweeps up the ashes, and deposits them in her cinder-pail, which is a japanned tin pail, with a wire-sifter inside, and a closely-fitting top. In this pail the cinders are sifted, and reserved for use in the kitchen or under the copper, the ashes only being thrown away. The cinders disposed of, she proceeds to black-lead the grate, producing the black lead, the soft brush for laying it on, her blacking and polishing brushes, from the box which contains her tools. This housemaid's box should be kept well stocked. Having blackened, brushed, and polished every part, and made all clean and bright, she now proceeds to lay the fire. Sometimes it is very difficult to get a proper polish to black grates, particularly if they have been neglected, and allowed to rust at all. But later on we give recipes for treating them that will be found useful.

Bright grates require unceasing attention to keep them in perfect order. A day should never pass without the housemaid rubbing with a dry leather the polished parts of a grate, as also the fender and fire-irons. A careful and attentive housemaid should have no occasion ever to use emery-paper for any part but the bars, which, of course, become blackened by the fire. (Some mistresses, to save labour, have a double set of bars, one set bright for the summer, and another black set to use when fires are in requisition.)

The several fires lighted, the housemaid proceeds with her dusting, and polishing the several pieces of furniture in the breakfast-parlour, leaving no corner unvisited. Before sweeping the carpet, it is a good practice to sprinkle it all over with tea-leaves, which not only lay all dust, but give a slightly fragrant smell to the room. It is now in order for the reception of the family; and where there is neither footman nor parlour-maid, she now proceeds to the dressing-room, and lights her mistress's fire, if she is in the habit of having one to dress by. Her mistress is called, hot water placed in the dressing-room for her use, her clothes—as far as they are under the housemaid's charge—put before the fire to air, hanging a fire-guard on the bars where there is one, while she proceeds to prepare the breakfast.

The housemaid's work in summer is considerably abridged: she throws open the windows of the several rooms not occupied as bedrooms, that they may receive the fresh morning air before they are occupied; she prepares the breakfast-room by sweeping the carpet, rubbing tables and chairs, dusting mantel-shelf and picture-frames with a light brush, dusting the furniture, and beating and sweeping the rug; she cleans the grate when necessary, and replaces the white paper or arranges the shavings with which it is filled, leaving everything clean and tidy for breakfast. It is not enough, however, in cleaning furniture, just to pass lightly over the surface; the rims and legs of tables, and the backs and legs of chairs and sofas, should be rubbed vigorously daily; if there is a book-case, every corner of every pane and ledge requires to be carefully wiped, so that not a speck of dust can be found in the room.

Morning Work.—After the breakfast-room is finished, the housemaid should proceed to sweep down the stairs, commencing at the top, whilst the cook has the charge of the hall, door-step, and passages. After this she should go into the drawing-room, cover up every article of furniture that is likely to spoil, with large dusting-sheets, and put the chairs together, by turning them seat to seat, and, in fact, make as much room as possible, by placing all the loose furniture in the middle of the room, whilst she sweeps the corners and sides. When this is accomplished, the furniture can then be put back in its place, and the middle of the room swept, sweeping the dirt, as before said, towards the fireplace. The same rules should be observed in cleaning the drawing-room grates as we have just stated, putting down the cloth, before commencing, to prevent the carpet from getting soiled. In the country, a room would not require sweeping thoroughly like this more than twice a week; but the housemaid should go over it every morning with a dust-pan and broom, taking up every crumb and piece she may see. After the sweeping she should leave the room, shut the door, and proceed to lay the breakfast. Where there is neither footman nor parlour-maid kept, the duty of laying the breakfast-cloth rests on the housemaid.

Laying the Cloth for Breakfast.—The heater of the tea-urn is to be placed in the hottest part of the kitchen fire; or, where the kettle is used, boiled on the kitchen fire, and then removed to the parlour, where it is kept hot. Having washed herself free from the dust arising from the morning's work, the housemaid collects the breakfast-things on her tray, takes the breakfast-cloth from the napkin press, and carries them all on the tray into the parlour; arranges them on the table, placing a sufficiency of knives, forks, and salt-cellars for the family, and takes the tray back to the pantry; gets a supply of milk, cream, and bread; fills the butter-dish, taking care that the salt is plentiful, and soft and dry, and that hot plates and egg-cups are ready where warm meat or eggs are served, and that butter-knife and bread-knife are in their places. And now she should give the signal for breakfast, holding herself ready to fill the urn with hot water, or hand the kettle, and take in the rolls, toast, and other eatables, with which the cook supplies her, when the breakfast-room bell rings; bearing in mind that she is never to enter the parlour with dirty hands or with a dirty apron, and that everything is to be handed on a tray; that she is to hand everything she may be required to supply, on the left hand of the person she is serving, and that all is done quietly and without bustle or hurry. In some families, where there is a large number to attend on, the cook waits at breakfast whilst the housemaid is busy upstairs in the bedrooms, or sweeping, dusting, and putting the drawing-room in order.

Bedroom Work.—Breakfast served, the housemaid proceeds to the bed-chambers, throws up the sashes, if not already done, pulls up the blinds, throwing back curtains at the same time, and opens the beds, by removing the clothes, placing them over a horse, or, failing that, over the backs of chairs. She now proceeds to empty the slops. In doing this, everything is emptied into the slop-pail, leaving a little scalding-hot water for a minute in such vessels as require it; adding a drop of turpentine to the water, when that is not sufficient to cleanse them. The basin is emptied, well rinsed with clean water, and carefully wiped; the ewers emptied and washed; finally, the water-jugs themselves emptied out and rinsed, and wiped dry. As soon as this is done, she should remove and empty the pails, taking care that they also are well washed, scalded, and wiped as soon as they are empty. Next follows bedmaking, at which the cook or kitchen-maid, where one is kept, usually assists; but, before beginning, velvet chairs, or other things injured by dust, should be removed to another room. In bedmaking, the fancy of its occupant should be consulted; some like beds sloping from the top towards the feet, swelling slightly in the middle; others, perfectly flat: a good housemaid will accommodate each bed to the taste of the sleeper, taking care to shake, beat, and turn it well in the process. Some persons prefer sleeping on the mattress; in which case a feather bed is usually beneath, resting on a second mattress, and a straw paillasse at the bottom. In this case, the mattresses should change places daily; the feather bed placed on the mattress shaken, beaten, taken up and opened several times, so as thoroughly to separate the feathers: if too large to be thus handled, the maid should shake and beat one end first, and then the other, smoothing it afterwards equally all over into the required shape, and place the mattress gently over it. Any feathers which escape in this process a tidy servant will put back through the seam of the tick; she will also be careful to sew up any stitch that gives way the moment it is discovered. The bedclothes are laid on, beginning with an under blanket and sheet, which are tucked under the mattress at the bottom. The bolster is then beaten and shaken, and put on, the top of the sheet rolled round it, and the sheet tucked in all round. The pillows and other bedclothes follow, and the counterpane over all, which should fall in graceful folds, and at equal distance from the ground all round. The curtains are drawn to the head and folded neatly across the bed, and the whole finished in a smooth and graceful manner. Where spring-mattresses are used, care should be taken that the top one is turned every day. The housemaid should now take up in a dustpan any pieces that may be on the carpet; she should dust the room, shut the door, and proceed to another room. When all the bedrooms are finished, she should dust the stairs, and polish the handrail of the banisters, and see that all ledges, window-sills, &c., are quite free from dust. It will be necessary for the housemaid to divide her work, so that she may not have too much to do on certain days, and not sufficient to fill up her time on other days. In the country, bedrooms should be swept and thoroughly cleaned once a week; and to be methodical and regular in her work, the housemaid should have certain days for doing certain rooms thoroughly. For instance, the drawing-room on Monday, two bedrooms on Tuesday, two on Wednesday, and so on, reserving a day for thoroughly cleaning the plate, bedroom candlesticks, &c. &c., which she will have to do where there is no parlour-maid or footman kept. By this means the work will be divided, and there will be no unnecessary bustling and hurrying, as is the case where the work is done any time, without rule or regulation.

Weekly Work.—Once a week, when a bedroom is to be thoroughly cleaned, the housemaid should commence by brushing the mattresses of the bed before it is made; she should then make it, shake the curtains, lay them smoothly on the bed, and pin or tuck up the bottom valance, so that she may be able to sweep under the bed. She should then unloop the window-curtains, shake them, and pin them high up out of the way. After clearing the dressing-table, and the room altogether of little articles of china, &c. &c., she should shake the toilet-covers, fold them up, and lay them on the bed, over which a large dusting-sheet should be thrown. She should then sweep the room; first of all sprinkling the carpet with well-squeezed tea-leaves, or a little freshly-pulled grass, when this is obtainable. After the carpet is swept, and the grate cleaned, she should wash with soap and water, with a little soda in it, the washing-table apparatus, removing all marks or fur round the jugs, caused by the water. The water-bottles and tumblers must also have her attention, as well as the top of the washing-stand, which should be cleaned with soap and flannel if it be marble: if of polished mahogany, no soap must be used. When these are all clean and arranged in their places, the housemaid should scrub the floor where it is not covered with carpet, under the beds, and round the wainscot. She should use as little soap and soda as possible, as too free a use of these articles is liable to give the boards a black appearance. In the country, cold soft water, a clean scrubbing-brush, and a willing arm, are all that are required to make bedroom floors look white. In winter it is not advisable to scrub rooms too often, as it is difficult to dry them thoroughly at that season of the year, and nothing is more dangerous than to allow persons to sleep in a damp room. The housemaid should now dust the furniture, blinds, ornaments, &c.; polish the looking-glass; arrange the toilet-cover and muslin; remove the cover from the bed, and straighten and arrange the curtains and counterpane. A bedroom should be cleaned like this every week. There are times, however, when it is necessary to have the carpet up; this should be done once a year in the country, and twice a year in large cities. The best time for these arrangements is spring and autumn, when the bed-furniture requires changing to suit the seasons of the year. After arranging the furniture, it should all be well rubbed and polished; and for this purpose the housemaid should provide herself with an old silk pocket-handkerchief, to finish the polishing. As modern furniture is now nearly always French-polished, it should often be rubbed with an old silk rubber, or a fine cloth or duster, to keep it free from smears. Three or four times a year any of the following polishes may be applied with very great success, as any of them make French-polished furniture look very well. One precaution must be taken,—not to put too much of the polish on at one time, and *to rub, not smear* it over the articles.

Lamp Cleaning.—The chamber candlesticks should be brought down and cleaned, the parlour lamps trimmed—and here the housemaid's utmost care is required. In cleaning candlesticks, as in every other cleaning, she should have cloths and brushes kept for that purpose alone; the knife used to scrape them should be applied to no other purpose; the tallow-grease should be thrown into a box kept for the purpose; the same with everything connected with the lamp-trimming; the best mode of doing which she may learn from directions given with different lamps, always bearing in mind, however, that without perfect cleanliness, which involves occasional scalding, no lamp can be kept in order. After scalding a lamp, it should be rinsed out with a little spirits; this will prevent the oil sputtering on first being lighted after the scalding.

The drawing and dining-room, inasmuch as everything there is more costly and valuable, require even more care. When the carpets are of the kind known as velvet-pile, they require to be swept firmly by a hard whisk brush, made of cocoanut fibre. The furniture must be carefully gone over in every corner with a soft cloth, that it may be left perfectly free from dust; or where that is beyond reach, with a brush made of long feathers, or a goose's wing. The sofas are swept in the same manner, slightly beaten, the cushions shaken and smoothed, the picture-frames swept, and everything arranged in its proper place. This, of course, applies to dining as well as drawing-room and morning-room. And now the housemaid may dress herself for the day, and prepare for the family dinner, at which she must attend, should there be no parlour-maid, or should she be required to assist the latter.

Evening Duties.—In summer-time the windows of all the bedrooms, which have been closed during the heat of the day, should be thrown open for an hour or so after sunset, in order to air them. Before dark they should be closed, the bedclothes turned down, and the night-clothes laid in order for use when required. During winter, where fires are required in the dressing-rooms, they should be lighted an hour before the usual time of retiring, placing a fireguard before each fire. At the same time, the night-things on the horse should be placed before it to be aired, with a tin can of hot water, if the mistress is in the habit of washing before going to bed. We may add, that there is no greater preservative of beauty than washing the face every night in hot water. The housemaid will probably be required to assist her mistress to undress and put her dress in order for the morrow; in which case her duties are very much those of the lady's-maid. And now the fire is made up for the night, the fireguard replaced, and everything in the room in order for the night, the housemaid taking care to leave the night-candle and matches together in a convenient place, should they be required. It is usual in summer to remove all highly fragrant flowers from sleeping-rooms, the impression being that their scent is injurious in a close chamber. On leisure days, the housemaid should be able to do some needlework for her mistress,—such as turning and mending sheets and darning the house linen, or assist her in anything she may think fit to give her to do. For this reason it is almost essential that a housemaid, in a small family, should be an expert needlewoman; as, if she be a good manager and an active girl, she will have time on her hands to get through plenty of work.

Periodical Cleanings.—Besides the daily routine which we have described, there are portions of every house which can only be thoroughly cleaned occasionally; at which time the whole house usually undergoes a more thorough cleaning than is permitted in the general way. On these occasions it is usual to begin at the top of the house and clean downwards; moving everything out of the room; washing the wainscoting or paint with soft soap and water; pulling down the beds and thoroughly cleansing all the joints; "scrubbing" the floor; beating feather beds, mattress, and paillasse, and thoroughly purifying every article of furniture before it is put back in its place.

Spring Cleaning.—This general cleaning usually takes place in the spring or early summer, when the warm curtains of winter are replaced by the light and cheerful muslin curtains. Carpets are at the same time taken up and beaten, except where the mistress of the house has been worried into an experiment by the often-reiterated question, "Why beat your carpets?" In this case she will probably have made up her mind to try the cleaning process, and arranged with the company to send for them on the morning when cleaning commenced. It is hardly necessary to repeat, that on this occasion every article is to be gone over, the French-polished furniture well rubbed and polished. The same thorough system of cleaning should be done throughout the house; the walls cleaned where painted, and swept down with a soft broom or feather brush where papered; the window and bed curtains, which have been replaced with muslin ones, carefully brushed, or, if they require it, cleaned; lamps not likely to be required, washed out with hot water, dried, and cleaned. The several grates should be furnished with their summer ornaments.

As winter approaches, this house-cleaning will have to be repeated, and the warm bed and window curtains replaced. The process of scouring and cleaning is again necessary, and must be gone through, beginning at the top, and going through the house, down to the kitchens.

Occasional Work.—Independently of these daily and periodical cleanings, other occupations will present themselves from time to time, which the housemaid will have to perform. When spots show on polished furniture, they can generally be restored by soap-and-water and a sponge, the polish being brought out by using a little polish, and then well rubbing it. Again, drawers which draw out stiffly may be made to move more easily if the spot where they press is rubbed over with a little soap.

Chips broken off any of the furniture should be collected and replaced, by means of a little glue applied to it. Liquid glue, which is sold prepared in bottles, is very useful to have in the house, as it requires no melting; and anything broken can be so quickly repaired.

Breaking glass and china is about the most disagreeable thing that can happen in a family, and it is, probably, a greater annoyance to a right-minded servant than to the mistress. A neat-handed housemaid may sometimes repair these breakages, where they are not broken in very conspicuous places, by joining the pieces very neatly together with a cement for which we give a recipe.

These are the duties of the housemaid or housemaids, and according to the number kept so will the work be divided between them, every household having different rules and management.

THE HOUSEMAID.

DUTIES OF THE LADY'S-MAID

The duties of a lady's-maid are more numerous, and perhaps more onerous, than those of the valet; for while the latter is aided by the tailor, the hatter, the linen-draper, and the perfumer, the lady's-maid has to originate many parts of the mistress's dress herself: she should, indeed, be a tolerably expert milliner and dressmaker, a good hairdresser, and possess some chemical knowledge of the cosmetics with which the toilet-table is supplied, in order to use them with safety and effect. Her first duty in the morning, after having performed her own toilet, is to examine the clothes put off by her mistress the evening before, either to put them away, or to see that they are all in order to put on again. During the winter, and in wet weather, the dresses should be carefully examined, and the mud removed. Dresses of tweed, and other woollen materials, may be laid out on a table and brushed all over; but in general, even in woollen fabrics, the lightness of the tissues renders brushing unsuitable to dresses, and it is better to remove the dust from the folds by beating them lightly with a handkerchief or thin cloth. Silk dresses should never be brushed, but rubbed with a piece of merino, or other soft material, of a similar colour, kept for the purpose. Summer dresses of barège, muslin, mohair, and other light materials, simply require shaking; but if the muslin be tumbled, it must be ironed afterwards. If the dresses require slight repair, it should be done at once: "a stitch in time saves nine."

The bonnet should be dusted with a light feather plume, in order to remove every particle of dust; but this has probably been done, as it ought to have been, the night before. Velvet bonnets, and other velvet articles of dress, should be cleaned with a soft brush. If the flowers with which the bonnet is decorated have been crushed or displaced, or the leaves tumbled, they should be raised and readjusted by means of flower-pliers. If feathers have suffered from damp, they should be held near the fire for a few minutes, and restored to their natural state by the hand or a soft brush.

The Chausserie, or foot-gear of a lady, is one of the few things left to mark her station, and requires special care. Satin boots or shoes should be dusted with a soft brush, or wiped with a cloth. Kid or varnished leather should have the mud wiped off with a sponge charged with milk, which preserves its softness and polish. The following is also an excellent polish for applying to ladies' boots, instead of blacking them:—Mix equal proportions of sweet-oil, vinegar, and treacle, with 1 oz. of lamp-black. When all the ingredients are thoroughly incorporated, rub the mixture on the boots with the palm of the hand, and put them in a cool place to dry. Ladies' blacking, which may be purchased in 6d, and 1s. bottles, is also very much used for patent leather and kid boots, particularly when they are a little worn. This blacking is merely applied with a piece of sponge, and the boots should not be put on until the blacking is dry und hardened.

These various preliminary offices performed, the lady's-maid should prepare for dressing her mistress, arranging her dressing-room, toilet-table, and linen, according to her mistress's wishes and habits. The details of dressing we need not touch upon,—every lady has her own mode of doing so; but the maid should move about quietly, perform any offices about her mistress's person, as lacing stays, gently, and adjust her linen smoothly.

Having prepared the dressing-room by lighting the fire, sweeping the hearth, and made everything ready for dressing her mistress, placed her linen before the fire to air, and laid out the various articles of dress she is to wear, which will probably have been arranged the previous evening, the lady's-maid is prepared for the morning's duties.

Hairdressing is the most important part of the lady's-maid's office. If ringlets are worn, remove the curl-papers, and, after thoroughly brushing the back hair both above and below, dress it according to the prevailing fashion. If bandeaux are worn, the hair is thoroughly brushed and frizzed outside and inside, folding the hair back round the head, brushing it perfectly smooth, giving it a glossy appearance by the use of pomades, or oil, applied by the palm of the hand, smoothing it down with a small brush dipped in bandoline. Double bandeaux are formed by bringing most of the hair forward, and rolling it over frizettes made of hair the same colour as that of the wearer: it is finished behind by plaiting the hair, and arranging it in such a manner as to look well with the head-dress.

Lessons in hairdressing may be obtained, and at not an unreasonable charge. If a lady's-maid can afford it, we would advise her to initiate herself in the mysteries of hairdressing before entering on her duties. If a mistress finds her maid handy, and willing to learn, she will not mind the expense of a few lessons, which are almost necessary, as the fashion and mode of dressing the hair is so continually changing. Brushes and combs should be kept scrupulously clean, by washing them about twice a week: to do this oftener spoils the brushes, as very frequent washing makes them so very soft.

RECIPES FOR THE LADY'S MAID

TREATMENT OF THE HAIR

The Germans, who are noted for the length and quantity of their hair, recommend the following treatment:—Twice a month wash the head with a quart of soft water, in which a handful of bran has been boiled, and in which a little white soap has been dissolved. Next rub the yolk of an egg, slightly beaten, into the roots of the hair, let it remain a few minutes, and wash it off thoroughly with pure water, rinsing the head well. Wipe and rub the hair dry with a towel, and comb the hair up from the head, parting it with the fingers. If the hair has been very dry *before* the washing, a little pomatum should be used.

TO MAKE POMADE FOR THE HAIR

Ingredients.—¼ lb. of lard, 2 pennyworth of castor-oil; scent.

Mode.—Let the lard be unsalted; beat it up well; then add the castor-oil, and mix thoroughly together with a knife, adding a few drops of any scent that may be preferred. Put the pomatum into pots, which keep well covered to prevent it turning rancid.

AN EXCELLENT POMATUM

Ingredients.—1½ lb. of lard, ½ pint of olive-oil, ½ pint of castor-oil, 4 oz. of spermaceti, bergamot, or any other scent; elder-flower water.

Mode.—Wash the lard well in the elder-flower water; drain, and beat it to a cream. Mix the two oils together, and heat them sufficiently to dissolve the spermaceti, which should be beaten fine in a mortar. Mix all these ingredients together with the brandy and whatever kind of scent may be preferred; and whilst warm pour into glass bottles for use, keeping them well corked. The best way to liquefy the pomatum is to set the bottle in a saucepan of warm water. It will remain good for many months.

TO PROMOTE THE GROWTH OF HAIR

Ingredients.—Equal quantities of olive-oil and spirit of rosemary; a few drops of oil of nutmeg.

Mode.—Mix the ingredients together, rub the roots of the hair every night with a little of this liniment, and the growth of it will very soon sensibly increase. When illness is the cause of the loss of hair, brandy should be applied three times a week, and cold cream on the alternate nights.

TO WASH BRUSHES

Dissolve a piece of soda in some hot water, allowing a piece the size of a walnut to a quart of water. Put the water into a basin, and, after combing out the hair from the brushes, dip them, bristles downwards, into the water and out again, keeping the backs and handles as free from the water as possible. Repeat this until the bristles look clean; then rinse the brushes in a little cold water; shake them well, and wipe the handles and backs with a towel, *but not the bristles*, and set the brushes to dry in the sun, or near the fire; but take care not to put them too close to it. Wiping the bristles of a brush makes them soft, as does also the use of soap.

TO CLEAN COMBS

If it can be avoided, never wash combs, as the water often makes the teeth split, and the tortoiseshell or horn of which they are made, rough. Small brushes, manufactured purposely for cleaning combs, may be purchased at a trifling cost: with this the comb should be well brushed, and afterwards wiped with a cloth or towel.

CHAPPED HANDS

If the hands are washed in soft water with the best honey soap, and well rubbed dry with a soft towel, they need never be chapped. It is generally imperfect and careless washing which causes this inconvenience. When the hands are badly chapped, rub them two or three times a day with lemon-juice, or rub them over occasionally with an ointment made of fresh hog's-lard washed in rose or elder-flower water, a spoonful of honey, 2 spoonfuls of fine oatmeal well beaten up with the yolks of 2 new-laid eggs; or a useful mash for chapped hands may be made by adding 14 grains of sulphuric acid to 1 pint of rose-water and ½ oz. of oil of almonds, well shaken together, and when used diluted with a little water.

TO CLEAN FEATHERS

Cover the feathers with a paste made of pipe-clay and water, rubbing them one way only. When quite dry, shake off all the powder and curl with a knife. Grebe feathers may be washed with white soap in soft water.

TO RENEW VELVET

Hold the velvet, pile downwards, over boiling water, in which two pennyworth of stone ammonia is dissolved, double the velvet (pile inwards) and fold it lightly together.

TO CLEAN JEWELLERY

Jewels are generally wrapped up in cotton and kept in their cases; but they are subject to tarnish from exposure to the air and require cleaning. This is done by preparing clean soap-suds and using fine toilet-soap. Dip any article of gold, silver, gilt or precious stones into this lye, and dye them by brushing with a brush of soft badgers' hair, or a fine sponge; afterwards with a piece of fine cloth, and lastly, with a soft leather.

Gold or silver ornaments, and in general, all articles of jewellery, may be dressed by dipping them in spirits of wine warmed in a *bain-marie*, or shallow kettle, placed over a slow fire or hot plate. Silver ornaments should be kept in fine arrowroot, and completely covered with it.

DUTIES OF THE SICK-NURSE

All women are likely, at some period of their lives, to be called on to perform the duties of a sick-nurse, and should prepare themselves as much as possible, by observation and reading, for the occasion when they may be required to perform the office. The main requirements are good temper, compassion for suffering, sympathy with sufferers, which most women worthy of the name possess, neat-handedness, quiet manners, love of order, and cleanliness. With these qualifications there will be very little to be wished for; the desire to relieve suffering will inspire a thousand little attentions, and surmount the disgusts which some of the offices attending the sick-room are apt to create. Where serious illness visits a household, and protracted nursing is likely to become necessary, a professional nurse will probably be engaged, who has been trained to its duties; but in some families, and those not a few let us hope, the ladies of the family would oppose such an arrangement as a failure of duty on their part. There is, besides, even when a professional nurse is ultimately called in, a period of doubt and hesitation, while disease has not yet developed itself, when the patient must be attended to; and, in these cases, some of the female servants of the establishment must give their attendance in the sick-room. There are, also, slight attacks of cold, influenza, and accidents in a thousand forms, to which all are subject, where domestic nursing becomes a necessity; where disease, though unattended with danger, is nevertheless accompanied by the nervous irritation incident to illness, and when all the attention of the domestic nurse becomes necessary.

In the first stage of sickness, while doubt and a little perplexity hang over the household as to the nature of the sickness, there are some things about which no doubt can exist: the patient's room must be kept in a perfectly pure state, and arrangements made for proper attendance; for the first canon of nursing, according to Florence Nightingale, its apostle, is to "keep the air the patient breathes as pure as the external air, without chilling him." This can be done without any preparation which might alarm the patient; with proper windows, open fireplaces, and a supply of fuel, the room may be as fresh as it is outside, and kept at a temperature suitable for the patient's state.

Windows, however, must be opened from above, and not from below, and draughts avoided; cool air admitted beneath the patient's head chills the lower strata and the floor. The careful nurse will keep the door shut when the window is open; she will also take care that the patient is not placed between the door and the open window, nor between the open fireplace and the window. If confined to bed, she will see that the bed is placed in a thoroughly ventilated part of the room, but out of the current of air which is produced by the momentary opening of doors, as well as out of the line of draught between the window and the open chimney, and that the temperature of the room is kept about 64°. Where it is necessary to admit air by the door, the windows should be closed; but there are few circumstances in which good air can be obtained through the chamber-door; through it, on the contrary, the gases generated in the lower parts of the house are likely to be drawn into the invalid chamber.

These precautions taken, and plain nourishing diet, such as the patient desires, furnished, probably little more can be done, unless more serious symptoms present themselves; in which case medical advice will be sought.

Under no circumstances is ventilation of the sick-room so essential as in cases of febrile diseases, usually considered infectious; such as typhus and puerperal fevers, influenza, hooping-cough, small—and chicken-pox, scarlet fever, measles, and erysipelas: all these are considered communicable through the air; but there is little danger of infection being thus communicated, provided the room is kept thoroughly ventilated. On the contrary, if this essential be neglected, the power of infection is greatly increased and concentrated in the confined and impure air; it settles upon the clothes of the attendants and visitors, especially where they are of wool, and is frequently communicated to other families in this manner.

Under all circumstances, therefore, the sick-room should be kept as fresh and sweet as the open air, while the temperature is kept up by artificial heat, taking care that the fire burns clear, and gives out no smoke into the room; that the room is perfectly clean, wiped over with a damp cloth every day, if boarded; and swept, after sprinkling with damp tea-leaves, or other aromatic leaves, if carpeted; that all utensils are emptied and cleaned as soon as used, and not once in four-and-twenty hours, as is sometimes done. "A slop-pail," Miss Nightingale says, "should never enter a sick-room; everything should be carried direct to the water-closet, emptied there, and brought up clean; in the best hospitals the slop-pail is unknown." "I do not approve," says Miss Nightingale, "of making housemaids of nurses,— that would be waste of means; but I have seen surgical sisters, women whose hands were worth to them two or three guineas a week, down on their knees, scouring a room or hut, because they thought it was not fit for their patients: these women had the true nurse spirit."

Bad smells are sometimes met by sprinkling a little liquid chloride of lime on the floor; fumigation by burning pastiles is also a common expedient for the purification of the sick-room. They are useful, but only in the sense hinted at by the medical lecturer, who commenced his lecture thus:—"Fumigations, gentlemen, are of essential importance; they make so abominable a smell, that they compel you to open the windows and admit fresh air." In this sense they are useful, but ineffectual unless the cause be removed, and fresh air admitted.

The sick-room should be quiet; no talking, no gossiping, and, above all, no whispering,—this is absolute cruelty to the patient; he thinks his complaint the subject, and strains his ear painfully to catch the sound. No rustling of dresses, nor creaking shoes either; where the carpets are taken up, the nurse should wear list shoes, or some other noiseless material, and her dress should be of soft material that does not rustle. Miss Nightingale denounces crinoline, and quotes Lord Melbourne on the subject of women in the sick-room, who said, "I would rather have men about me, when ill, than women; it requires very strong health to put up with women." Ungrateful man! but absolute quiet is necessary in the sick-room.

Never let the patient be waked out of his first sleep by noise, never roused by anything like a surprise. Always sit in the apartment, so that the patient has you in view, and that it is not necessary for him to turn in speaking to you. Never keep a patient standing; never speak to one while moving. Never lean on the sick-bed. Above all, be calm and decisive with the patient, and prevent all noises over-head.

A careful nurse, when a patient leaves his bed, will open the sheets wide, and throw the clothes back so as thoroughly to air the bed; She will avoid drying or airing anything damp in the sick-room.

Diet suitable for patients will depend, in some degree, on their natural likes and dislikes, which the nurse will do well to acquaint herself with. Beef tea is useful and relishing, but possesses little nourishment; when evaporated, it presents a teaspoonful of solid meat to a pint of water. Eggs are not equivalent to the same weight of meat. Arrowroot is less nourishing than flour. Butter is the lightest and most digestible kind of fat. Cream, in some diseases, cannot be replaced. But, to sum up with some of Miss Nightingale's useful maxims:—Observation is the nurse's best guide, and the patient's appetite the rule. Half a pint of milk is equal to a quarter of a pound of meat. Beef tea is the least nourishing food administered to the sick; and tea and coffee, she thinks, are both too much excluded from the sick-room.

THE SICK-NURSE.

RECIPES FOR THE SICK-NURSE

BRAN POULTICE

Place the quantity of bran required, according to the size of the poultice, upon the top of the boiling water, and when the heat has penetrated the bran, stir it gently in. Pour off the superabundant water, and apply the poultice as hot as it can be borne.

OINTMENT FOR CHAPPED HANDS

Ingredients.—1 oz. of bitter almonds, oil of sweet almonds, the yolk of 1 egg, and a little tincture of benzoin; 10 drops of oil of caraway.

Mode.—Blanch the almonds, beat them to a paste by working in gradually the oil of sweet almonds and the egg, also the benzoin and oil of caraway, so as to make the ointment of the consistence of thick cream. Before going to bed, the hands should be well washed with soap and warm soft water, and the ointment rubbed well into them. It is desirable to keep the hands covered with a pair of soft kid gloves while the ointment is upon them. Another ointment can be made with Goulard's extract, 1 fluid drachm; rose-water, 1 fluid oz.; spermaceti ointment, 2 oz. Melt the ointment, and rub it up with the extract of Goulard mixed with the rose-water.

POULTICE FOR CHILBLAINS

Bake a common white turnip and scrape out the pulp; mix it with a tablespoonful of salad-oil, one of mustard, and one of grated horseradish. In this way form a poultice and apply it to the chilblains on a piece of linen rag.

TO CURE A COLD

(A Most Efficacious and Simple Remedy for a Severe Cold in the Head)

Take a small basin, put into it boiling water and strong camphorated spirit, in the proportion of 1 teaspoonful of spirit to ½ pint of water. Wring out a sponge in this as hot as possible, and apply it to the nose or mouth; draw in the steam with the nose first and then with the mouth; swallow the steam, and, to prevent any escape, cover the head with a flannel. Repeat this operation for some time, having another hot sponge when the first gets cool. Sponges so wrung out in the same mixture may with great benefit be applied outwards to the throat and chest.

Camphorated salvolatile is a good medicine for a cold, 30 drops in a wineglass of warm water several times in the course of the day.

TO APPLY LEECHES

Should they not bite at once put the spot of blood obtained by a slight prick of the finger on the place. When filled they usually roll off; but if it is necessary to detach them they must not be pulled, but a little salt must be shaken over them, which will make them release their hold. Should too much bleeding follow apply a little powdered alum.